Snapshots In Time

THE S&G RAILROAD

Robert Michaels

Text Copyright © 2013 Robert Michaels

ISBN: 1490924434

ISBN 13: 9781490924434

Library of Congress Control Number: 2013912750

CreateSpace Independent Publishing Platform

North Charleston, South Carolina

DEDICATION

To Samy

Snapshots In Time

THE S&G RAILROAD

Table of Contents

A PERSONAL NOTE
TO MY READERS

The story you are about to read is true. Do not let the love, sense of wonder or imagination deceive you. The fun, mystery, and adventure we are about to share with you, are an integral part of an extraordinary story you are certain to identify with. They will uplift your spirit, and will motivate you as well.

Before I began our adventure, I thought I knew most of what it took to be a parent or grandparent. After all, I had raised two children, and spent over thirty years as a teacher in the public school system. I received numerous awards at the local, state, and national level for outstanding achievement! I now know I had more to learn.

The overwhelming majority of us want to improve our great country, and protect, nurture, and love our most precious resource, our children. We must recognize what they need most is our time.

The original manuscript was written for the express purpose of chronicling our journey together. My intention was to leave something behind so that my grandson would always remember the great and memorable times we had together. We are now sharing our journey through time with you.

Finally, this book like our journey does not end on the last page. In many ways it never ends. You are encouraged to "read between the lines" as we share our journey with you. We all have something unique to contribute to the physical, emotional, spiritual, and educational growth of our children!

These are the "snapshots in time" we will cherish forever.

Robert Michaels

Snapshots in Time - The S&G Railroad Book I

sgintime.com

> *"Tell me and I will forget. Teach me and I will remember. Involve me and I will learn."*
>
> BENJAMIN FRANKLIN

Introduction

Something extremely special happened on that cold winter day. A series of events was about to be set in motion that would enhance our relationship with one another, and strengthen the bond between us. These events proved impossible to foresee nor do we fully understand all of them now. Our journey would surprise us at every turn and together we enjoyed "expecting the unexpected". We had unlocked a portal that led us to explore the past, present and future! Samy and I looked forward every day to the mystery, suspense, adventures and the challenges our journey together consistently presented.

Our story changed not only our relationship with one another, but also the way we viewed the past, present and future. It is a very personal, exciting, and imaginative journey, and one we truly hope will never end. Our journey represents a unique and significant opportunity for children, parents, grandparents, or anyone in a position to influence a child in a positive way, to learn, create, and grow together. The journey we take together represents a time capsule, that when opened, generates opportunities that will lead you to places you may never have imagined. We hope it will open your heart and your mind to the limitless possibilities our journey has presented to us.

The story of our journey together as well as our relationship with one another is at the very core of the dreams we have for our children. The love we have for them and our desire to see them grow and realize their full potential is an integral part of the journey. If you are a parent, grandparent or a grandchild you will identify and relate to the journey we are about to share with you. We are confident you will enjoy it and we hope it will inspire you as well.

The author has a great deal of experience working with young people. He was a highly decorated educator in the public school system for over thirty years. His experience in creating projects and experiences for young people is quite substantial. Clearly, no amount of experience prepared him for the privilege of becoming a grandparent. There are no words to express accurately the real substance of his relationship with his grandson and their love for one another.

There is no greater feeling than contributing to something greater than yourself. There is no greater gift you can give than your time. We all have too little of it and it is imperative that we make productive use of it. When we set goals or priorities, who among us would not include our children and grandchildren?

Now more than ever our children and grandchildren need our time. Too many negative influences exist and making the youngest in our society our number one priority is paramount. The profound effect that you have on your child or grandchild should never be underestimated. Should you be in a position to be a positive influence in a child's development and not have children of your own, you will find our journey uplifting and enjoyable as well. Whatever your circumstances you can make a difference in their lives!

Today, the reader has literally tens of thousands of books to choose from on a variety of different topics. Our "journey" together offers the reader an opportunity to select a topic that is not relevant to a select few, but to all of us. This is a significant opportunity to share something with the most important people in our lives, our children, and grandchildren. We need, now more than ever, true stories that are uplifting to the human spirit, good for the soul and do not include the sensationalism, violence, and pessimism we seem to find everywhere.

§

How often have we said or thought that our children grow up much too quickly? Bedtime stories we enjoyed reading and our children loved to hear suddenly become "childish," toys are "outgrown," and much of what we associate with childhood fades much too fast. How many times have we looked at our children and grandchildren and said, "I'd like you to stay just as you are now." This is one of many reasons that when we find ourselves with an opportunity that will allow our children to grow closer to family, and encourage educational and value-oriented opportunities we should seize them.

The very nature of these "snapshots in time" is what makes them so powerful in every way. The journey we are about to begin together is an extraordinary compilation of those moments in time we will always remember. Our journey is "multi-generational" and brings us back in time and into the future as well. If we were sure of anything it was that, it would create memories that would remain in our hearts forever.

Our children and grandchildren can learn valuable lessons from the past, and gain knowledge through opportunities we provide for them. They can do so under the guidance and love of the most experienced teachers in the world, their parents and grandparents! Children have an abundance of creative problem-solving skills that become evident when we involve them in educational and memorable activities. I was committed to achieving all of the above while capitalizing on our newly-found common interest.

The S & G Railroad is about the love a grandfather and grandson share. The bond between them grows stronger with every passing day. Our journey together is one adventure after another and may lead you to the conclusion that "the more things change the more they stay the same." Or do they?

We were not aware of it that day, but this was just the beginning. It was to be the beginning of an adventure that neither Samy nor I had envisioned. Our journey would span over one hundred and fifty years! You will find yourself at the turn of the century during the "Golden Age" of railroads, exploring the woods in the 1950s, on several "expeditions" in the present, and propelled briefly into the future!

> *"With time many of the facts I learned were forgotten,*
> *but I never lost the excitement of discovery"*
>
> PAUL BERG

CHAPTER 1

The Excitement of Discovery

What caused Samy to walk down the upstairs hallway that day will always remain a mystery. He followed it into what used to be an old master bedroom suite complete with a large bath and walk-in closet. The room next to it was also a bedroom. Several years ago, the wall between the two rooms was removed and this bedroom was now a sitting room. He had been there before, but today a combination of adventure, mystery, and being five and one half years old led Samy to think differently about the possibilities these rooms offered, especially the master bedroom closet.

"Grandpa, I have a great idea, come in and see!" I immediately walked down the hallway from my office to see what my grandson's idea was. Samy was standing in the almost empty walk-in closet with a huge smile on his face. "Come in and shut the door and turn on the light, Grandpa." I walked in, turned on the light and sat down next to my grandson on a king-sized comforter that was being stored in the corner of the closet. "Isn't this a cool room and wouldn't this make a great secret clubhouse?"

"Really cool, I replied. Did you know that this is a solid steel and titanium door and the walls are lined with lead?" The sense of mystery in my voice made Samy giggle.

"They're not, but they could be, Grandpa. This could be the greatest clubhouse and we could even race cars in here."

"Sounds good to me, buddy, is there anything we need to do or are there any supplies we need?" I asked.

"Probably a couple of pillows, flashlights and maybe some extra batteries we could keep in those drawers." Samy pointed toward a three-drawer table positioned in the rear of the closet.

"Do you see those binders that are marked Photo Albums? They are classified documents that require a very high security clearance that only you and I have." As I looked up at the shelves I realized Samy immediately understood and he loved every minute of it.

The size of the space was perfect for Samy's plans. It measured approximately 8 feet by 6 feet and was equipped with a door that disappeared into the wall when opened. The feel of the carpet, combined with its size, and "security door," gave us the impression we were in a highly classified control room completely cut off from the rest of the world. Our control room even had interior lighting! On the shelves above were photo albums, which no doubt contained classified intelligence photographs. We had more than enough space to move around and it proved to be quite comfortable. There were only a few boxes being stored there; however, only one caught our attention. This box, though we did not know it at the time, would ignite the spark and provide the motivation to move us forward on a journey through the very fabric of the American experience. The nostalgia associated with our journey would bring us closer to and give us a better understanding of an era that was much more basic. We developed a passion for this period along with a love for the history and an appreciation for the people and events we would become acquainted with.

§

"Grandpa, what is in that box?" He pointed to a box in the corner of the closet. I did not remember when or how that box got there, but I was sure of one thing, it had been there for quite some time. The packing tape had almost disintegrated and the cardboard was extremely faded.

Little did we know that the contents of the box we were talking about would serve as the beginning of a journey that neither of us had planned that day as we talked about our new clubhouse. Establishing a clubhouse was our immediate goal, and we did not expect to find anything of any real interest inside of the closet.

We were about to be taken back in time over half a century, and we were caught completely by surprise! Our excitement began to grow and Samy's incredible sense of wonder kicked in quickly. His curiosity piqued when he saw how old the box appeared. The cardboard was faded and the packing tape use to seal the box showed its age.

"Grandpa, what could possibly be in this old box?" Samy repeated as he carefully pulled out the box and made a slit in the packing tape that age had made very easy to open. We discovered the contents were in another box housed inside the first. We could only imagine what this mystery box contained as we cautiously opened the outer box and painstakingly eased the inner box out. The inner box was halfway out and we spotted those magic words that have meant so much, to so many people, for so many years. I instantly found myself taken back in time 60 years! These words would soon provide the motivation to begin an incredible journey of our own.

There was little doubt that the words "Lionel Trains" which were now appearing have had the same effect along with the same fond memories for tens of thousands across the globe. I was now reliving a moment in time 60 years ago when I was close to Samy's age. It was extremely appropriate that I share this moment with my soon-to-be 6 year-old grandson. Frankly, I was not certain who was more excited! We carefully lifted out all of the parts we found in the box, with the same care our treasure was worthy of. We opened the Engine, Tender, Boxcar, Flatcar, Milk Car, and the Caboose. As we opened each box Samy's smile grew wider, his dimples deeper and his eyes twinkled with wonder. We became more excited as we opened each individual box. We had not found a toy but rather a piece of the past. It was as if a "portal" had opened allowing us to go back to 1950!

§

Upon closer examination of our treasure, we found that there were even a few accessories and a transformer. The Steam Engine and cars were in surprisingly good condition. "Grandpa, I don't think I've ever seen a train this detailed or one that looked so real," Samy said as if we had just entered the undiscovered tomb of an Egyptian Pharaoh. Within a half hour, we had the small oval of track set up. We were now waiting for the moment when we would find out whether our treasure from the 1950s still worked.

We attached the last wire to the transformer and turned on the main power switch. Samy slowly raised the lever on the transformer and the engine chugged and began to pull the cars around the track just as it did in 1950! "Wow! I can't believe it still works," Samy said excitedly. The sight before us mesmerized us both.

I felt an extreme sense of nostalgia rising inside of me. I was truly beginning to take that sentimental journey to a simpler time when I was Samy's age. I thought, "Could I have forgotten about these trains that I now remember so vividly?" The joy on my grandson's face brought me back to the present. I could not have been happier with our treasure and my grandson's reaction to it.

§

Trains have always fascinated people and they were working their "magic" on us that day. Perhaps it was the sense of nostalgia associated with them that often brought back memories of a simpler time.

We felt as if we had just returned from an archeological expedition where we had discovered the Holy Grail of archeology. Watching that 60-year-old train cruise around the track triggered many memories. Memories of the past, even though they took place 60 years ago, were extremely vivid. These moments we shared, would serve as a blueprint for the future for creating something very special together. There was no one I would rather share these memories with than my grandson.

I was surprised at how interested Samy was in the history of our "discovery." Samy was asking question after question about where the train set came from. "Did Santa leave this for you, Grandpa?" Samy asked, as he looked the engine over carefully.

I told him I was not sure whether Santa had left it for me or my mother and father had purchased it for my fifth birthday. I did remember it became a tradition to set it up around the Christmas tree each year. Exactly how many years that tradition lasted I was not sure.

"I really like this engine, Grandpa," Samy said as we watched it navigate the turns around the small oval of track while Samy pointed out every detail our new treasure possessed. We agreed that should we find that our engine needed anything we would make sure, that we would service it completely. By all observation, the engine and its cars looked great!

"I'm surprised it works as well as it does since it hasn't been oiled for over 50 years."

"Can you imagine not changing the oil on your car for sixty years, Grandpa?" Samy said while laughing.

Speaking of sixty year-old cars, I can remember my father's 1950 Chevrolet and I told my grandson who loved "everything cars" all about it. It was dark green with a white roof and going for a ride in it was always fun. "Do you think we could find that in a box somewhere?" I asked.

"I doubt that we will find your father's 1950 Chevrolet in a box, although I wish we could. The cars from the 1950's were really cool," Samy said showing those dimples that grew larger when he smiled.

§

"Did you know that my father worked for General Motors? They were the company that made Chevrolet, Pontiac, Oldsmobile, Buick, and Cadillac. My father, who is your great grandfather, worked in the factory that made the bearings for all the cars. He started out as a laborer working six huge machines and then became a supervisor. I remember the day we went to see the plant where he worked. It was the anniversary of General Motors making fifty-five million cars in 1955. During World War II, the same plant made the bearings for the tanks the military used during the war."

Samy was always interested in anything of an historical nature, especially when it concerned his family or local history. This fact about his family history was no different. His interest in all cars, past and present, together with his respect for family intrigued him. The fact that his grandfather's father was in some way responsible for helping the war effort and producing some of the old cars he loved, combined to make my revelation about my father much to interesting not to pursue. "Did your father fight in the war?" Samy asked.

"At that time there were jobs that were considered essential to the war effort and my father had one of these jobs. He was ready to go into the army until they found out what he did for a living. Making the bearings for tanks was considered a priority at that time and he worked long hours making them."

"Did you get to see the tanks?" Samy asked with a great deal of interest.

"The war ended before I was born so I didn't actually see the tanks, but I did see the huge bearings that went into the tanks a few years later. The biggest mistake our enemies made was to underestimate the manufacturing capability of the United States. Your great-grandfather was part of that effort along with millions of other Americans."

"Wow, I didn't know about any of that. You must have been proud of your father, Grandpa."

"I will always be proud of my father. He was very soft-spoken but above all, a good man who taught me many important things."

§

"As far as not changing the oil on a car for sixty years is concerned, Samy, you may be on to something, let's go on the computer, and look up maintenance for old trains. The older trains required oil and grease more often. The metal parts used to make our engine changed to a variety of different materials such as plastic. There is nothing wrong with plastic but should the engine fall or be dropped it will crack. Even some of the gears inside are now plastic and they certainly won't last as long."

Samy sat next to me and we typed in a few searches on the computer relating to old trains. We discovered a wealth of information related to the care and use of trains. Our research led us to a site that listed our engine! We learned that it was also an extremely rare model and might be worth quite a bit of money. When we searched for it by model number, serial number, and railway and we received no results. This confirmed its rarity.

"I wouldn't want to sell it no matter how much it is worth!" Samy said. He told me that having a train that I played with when I was his age was worth so much more. He told me that he watched a program on the History Channel that advised people to save all the original boxes, especially for "collectibles" because if you ever sold them they could be worth 2-3 times as much in the original boxes. He reiterated the fact that he would never sell our discovery for any amount of money. It was at that moment I realized that something special had indeed occurred today, and that this was just the beginning.

We looked at the diagrams and the places on the engine that required oil and parts that needed grease. Locating the appropriate oil and grease was easy as well. We ordered oil, grease, track, and wheel cleaner online and were on our way to eliminating any lubrication issues for our engine.

§

Samy and I watched that old engine pull the cars around the tracks for at least an hour that day. We talked about how "cool" trains were and how they changed people's lives at the turn of the century. "We should give our engine a name." Samy said.

"What did you have in mind for a name?" I asked.

"I know, let's call him 'Old Bob'!" Samy said excitedly.

"I would be honored and the name is very appropriate since it is after the original owner." At that moment, 1950 seemed like yesterday, and I knew exactly how my grandson felt at this moment in time. We were both happy to be able to share this "snapshot in time" together. We agreed at the first meeting in our "clubhouse" what our engine's name would be and that we would save the original boxes in case they were needed to transport the train from one place to another. This was one of those inexplicable moments that occur in all our lives that I felt I had indeed traveled back in time than back to the present. I also had the distinct feeling that the two were not very far apart after all!

"I think we should disconnect "Old Bob" until we oil and grease him completely, we wouldn't want anything to happen to him." I agreed that it was a good idea that we should not run "Old Bob" until we had serviced him the way the website we visited suggested. Samy's concern that we may damage our engine if we ran it without properly servicing it first was impressive.

"That is a very good idea, it is always better to be safe than sorry."

"We should put all the boxes away the way we found them?" Samy said with a determined look on his face when he was stacking all the boxes the individual train cars had come in.

"We should definitely keep the original boxes and put them away in the original outer box. The track and the train on it we can slide under the table so no one accidentally steps on them. Does that sound good to you?"

"As long as 'Old Bob' will be safe," Samy replied thoughtfully. Samy's concern for our recently discovered treasure was genuine and his enthusiasm and appreciation for the past sent a message that I could not ignore.

We carefully put the boxes the individual cars came in back in the cardboard box. Samy still could not get over that something as old as "Old Bob" could run as well and look as good as it did. To be able to relive an experience such as this was truly special. To be able to do so with my grandson was extraordinary!

§

Together we viewed at least a dozen magnificent layouts on the computer before the day ended. We found ourselves on several sites that displayed literally thousands of steam engines, diesel engines, boxcars, and accessories. I could see Samy's eyes growing wider with each page we looked at. I had to remind myself more than once, that if we were going to build something together, it meant much more than just "buying" something we found appealing. We knew without saying a word, that the journey we were about to embark upon together was something that would be "timeless" in the purest sense of the word.

The time we spent together, that day was very special to both of us and our treasure had generated a great deal of excitement. Our conversation about Samy's Great-Grandfather sparked an interest that he previously did not know he had. A great opportunity had presented itself, and as a Grandfather, I had a certain responsibility to take advantage of it. There would be many more occasions just like this one as we progressed further along on our journey together. What lay ahead of us existed only in our imagination and we would continue to build upon it until we had created something truly extraordinary that we would remember forever.

We may not have known it at the time, but a very powerful, educational, action-packed, adventurous, and memorable journey together had already begun. The memories we would create together would be the "snapshots in time" that would remain in our hearts forever.

"There are those who look at things the way they are and ask why...I dream things that never were, and ask why not"

Robert F. Kennedy

CHAPTER 2

𝔚𝔥𝔶 𝔑𝔬𝔱?

S amy and I had experienced the joy of watching that sixty-year-old steam engine make its way around the tracks, and we were both extremely happy that Samy wanted to name our engine "Old Bob" in honor of its owner in 1950. I had always been impressed with Samy's desire to learn about the history behind just about anything and "Old Bob" was no exception. His appetite for listening to stories about his family and their experiences when they were young was exceeded only by his desire to recreate them. This is probably the reason we had always joked about having a time machine complete with a "flux capacitor"!

"How about we jump into our time machine and go back to 1950 when "Old Bob" was making its way around the track for the first time?"

"We could take him back with us and he would be brand new," Samy said enthusiastically.

"I suppose that's true but then I would never have been able to play with him. Changing one event in the past could have a domino effect and change so much of the future. Our actions today change the future." I knew the intricacies of time travel with all its implications could give any one a headache just thinking about them.

"Neither would my mom when she was a little girl, so I guess we'll forget about the time machine for now Grandpa. Let's wait until we have it perfected and there are no bad effects from it. Maybe we can make an adjustment to our flux capacitor." Samy was clearly thinking about our discussion of how changing an event in the past could alter the future. "How can we change what is going to happen tomorrow or even next year?" Samy said quizzically.

I saw the look on my grandson's face at that moment and I knew he was giving serious thought to the time paradox. Everyone should be aware that the decisions we make today do alter the future. This is the essence of responsibility. The choices we make today will have a profound effect on our future. This is true for each of us as individuals and for our world as well. When we make decisions as individuals we affect not only our future, but countless others as well.

"I once read a story about a man who, in the early nineteen hundreds, was planning to make the journey from Europe to establish a home for himself in the United States. He went to the dock only to find out that the boat had sailed hours before his arrival. He was disappointed and did not try again until years later. There is another version of the story where this same man does not miss the boat and on the voyage to America, he meets a young woman, falls deeply in love with her, and they are later married. They settle in the United States and raise six children who in turn have children of their own. In the first version of this story generations of this family would not exist, but in the second version they would."

"I like the one where he doesn't miss the boat, because it seems happier," Samy said without hesitation.

"Suppose for a moment that he missed the boat but on his second attempt the boat had trouble at sea, and this man was responsible for saving the lives of several people?"

"Now I don't know which story I like because he saved people. In the first he was happy and had...this gets confusing!"

"It is supposed to be confusing, and fascinating at the same time. Time travel, or how one event affects another has been written about for years. You have to admit we have talked about a time machine and what we would do with it," I said with a smile.

"You know Grandpa we would not be here today talking about "Old Bob", trains or anything if..."

"If what?" I asked.

"If my Mom and Dad did not go to the same high school or you and Grandma decided to move to another town or..."

I saw that Samy was having what I call one of his "light bulb moments" and was amazed at how quickly my grandson picked up on what can be an extremely complex concept at any age.

"You are 100% right Samy, but they did go to the same school and Grandma and I didn't move and that is why I am so fortunate to be here with you now. I promise not to miss any boats if you will promise too."

"I promise to not miss any boats," Samy said as we both began to laugh.

"As far as playing with 'Old Bob' through our time machine and not being able to play with him, I think we should put that on hold for now."

§

Samy commented on the box cover art depicting a father with a dress shirt and tie on and his son with perfectly parted hair in typical 1950s fashion. The young boy on the cover also wore a tie. "What do you think about how the father and son are dressed?" I asked Samy.

"I guess it's OK, but I don't think you would find anyone dressed like that now."

"Probably not, times have changed along with hairstyles and the way people dress."

"Did your dad dress like that Grandpa?" Samy asked in a tone that exhibited a certain objectivity about how times have changed.

"As a matter of fact we both did and the picture of the boy on the box looks like me when I was close to your age."

We laughed and I explained the picture on the box was normal for that time period. The advertisers would put someone on the box who might buy their product. Sam looked up at me then looked toward the cover of the train box. He looked up again and picked up the cover and held it next to my head.

"Do you know what Grandpa?"

"What Samy?" I answered, never expecting what was to come next.

"Look at the color of this little boy's hair, this boy could have been you."

I examined the picture and sure enough the hair color was a good match and so were the freckles!

"Was your hair as red as the boy on the box?"

"Even more so, and it remained that way throughout high school. It became darker after college when it gradually became the color it is today. I guess you would call it auburn or reddish brown."

"At least you still have all of your hair. Most of my friends' Grandfathers are bald or grey and have really thin hair," Samy said in a very complimentary way.

"We thought your Mom was going to inherit my red hair but her hair became darker too. She does have my light complexion and so do you. Your hair is more blonde and we are not sure where that came from."

"My eyes are like yours, Grandpa."

"Mine are hazel which is a combination of green and brown. Your eyes are green and you inherited your father's eyes. I think you got the best from everyone."

"Oh Grandpa..."

"It is up to you to develop things like intelligence and the ability to distinguish right from wrong. Physical characteristics will not mean very much without the development of a strong moral compass," I said realizing at that moment Samy was only six.

Our discussion led us to talk about those things we inherit as well as those we do not. Samy's green eyes, dirty blonde hair, and athletic build have led his mother to say on many occasions that he is not dating until he is eighteen. Despite his strikingly handsome appearance and the compliments he receives, Samy is one of the most humble young boys I have met.

I tried on my varsity sweater from high school for Samy one day and surprisingly it still fit. Samy commented that I should be happy because not to many people look as young at my age. This is when I came to the conclusion that genes do skip a generation. This explains why Grandchildren and Grandparents get along so well. In any event, he is certainly good for my ego.

Our conversations on every topic have always been enjoyable. He possesses the sense of wonder so many of us lose, as we grow older. He has been blessed with a remarkable ability to relate to things past and present, that even most adults would find challenging or impossible. It is important we give all our children opportunities to display and develop these remarkable abilities.

§

We decided it was time for us to create a plan for what would become, even though we did not know it, an incredible journey together. I suggested that we make a list and put it down on paper. After much brainstorming, we came up with the following list that would serve as the blueprint for our project.

1. Measure the room we had selected as the home for our layout
2. Determine the actual size of the bench work or table
3. Decide what we wanted to include on our layout
4. Did we want the ability to run more than one train?
5. Would there be mountains?
6. How many levels?
7. Did we want one train to pass over another at some point(s)?
8. Did we want switching from one level to another?
9. Did we want a village with people, cars and houses?
10. Would there be any tunnels?

Samy was anxious to get started and he looked up at me and said, "Why don't we find a tape measure and see how big the room is?" We had selected the small bedroom as a potential home for our train layout, and I could see the excitement building in Samy's eyes. He was becoming more excited with each passing minute and I knew there was no turning back now. We found our tape measure and together we measured the room. The room measured twelve feet by thirteen feet and Samy recommended that we should leave at least one foot to be able to walk around our layout.

Grandma and Grandpa's house was a two story colonial with more than enough room for our train layout. The only room that was being used upstairs on a regular basis was my office. There was a bedroom dedicated specifically for Samy, the original master bedroom, and a third bedroom next to that. Since the interior partition wall separating the third bedroom and the original master bedroom had been taken down some years prior, there were walls on only three sides, and it was being used as a "sitting room."

We decided that the controls should be on the side without a wall. "Let's measure the track 'Old Bob' is on and this way we can see how much room we will need," Samy said energetically. When we did so we found that, the oval track "Old Bob" was on measured three and one half feet by two feet!

"If we make our layout 10 feet by 6 feet, it will be about three times longer and three times wider," I said.

"Wow Grandpa this layout will be really big! 'Old Bob' will get tired going around that track."

"When you are sixty years old you get tired going around the 'small' track," I said jokingly.

"You don't, Grandpa," Samy said with a serious tone in his voice.

"Don't what, Samy?"

"You don't get tired," Samy responded quickly.

"I can't, not if I'm going to keep up with you."

"Oh Grandpa..."

"What do you think? You are the chief architect on this project so if you have any suggestions about the size or anything else, make sure you make them known. "

"I think the size is great but we could make it so it goes around the entire next room too and that would be gigantic!" Samy had a big smile on his face and I couldn't help but think that if we did build around the adjoining room he would be ecstatic!

"Remember Samy we have to submit this to the local planning board and get it passed before we do anything else."

"What is a planning board?" Samy said looking somewhat perplexed.

"It is a group of people who decide if the proposed changes or additions you want to make on your house violate any existing building codes."

"When Daddy builds an addition to someone's house he gets a permit and has to build it a certain way before the inspectors come." Samy never ceases to amaze me and this time was no different.

"That is exactly right, Samy" I said with a combination of pride and amazement at my grandson's grasp of the subject. Knowledge of a subject is important however when and how to apply it is essential and I had no doubt that Samy would not have any difficulty with either.

"We don't have to have inspections or permits for a train layout, Grandpa," Samy responded with a question mark in his voice.

"We have a planning board and inspector all rolled up in one. When I tell you who it is you probably will be relieved even though you are somewhat apprehensive now."

"Who is our inspector?"

"Grandma is the inspector of course. She will have to give us the final approval on our plans after we submit our project description to her." Samy looked somewhat relieved at the prospect of Grandma giving us permission to go ahead with our plans. History had shown that there was not much Grandma would not do for Samy and the look on his face told me that Samy knew it also. Needless to say, he was confident having Grandma as our planning board and inspector.

At that point, we looked over the list we had made of those features we wanted to include on our layout. After looking at so many outstanding train layouts online, some of which took years to build, we definitely knew what we wanted. We wanted all of them rolled up into one! Never in a million years did either of us think our journey together would grow to include what it did and be as exciting!

§

We heard the sound of the garage door and Grandma coming in the garage after doing her food shopping. Samy said enthusiastically, "Let's go downstairs and ask Grandma what she thinks about our plans."

"That sounds like a good idea to me Samy, but take the list we have and you make our presentation to the planning board."

Samy was not the least bit reluctant to make our presentation. He quickly took our list downstairs and after helping Grandma with the bundles from the supermarket, began his presentation listing in detail everything we planned to do. Grandma listened to every word of her grandson's presentation, and later confessed that she would have bought anything he was selling. Samy was careful to include everything including the fact that we would relocate the loveseat, table, and television that presently resided in the room. He ended his presentation with "We promise we won't make a mess anywhere!"

There was no doubt in my mind what Grandma's reaction to Samy's project description would be. His excitement about what we were planning combined with his adorable smile, dimples, and wide-eyed enthusiasm made him, at least in my view, impossible to say no to. His grandmother listened carefully and when he was finished, there was a pause before Grandma spoke. Samy has always amazed us with his ability to turn on the charm and today was no exception. The pause we had detected was not because she was reluctant to give us the green light, but because she was stunned for a moment. Her grandson's presentation was so eloquent and thorough for a six year old that she needed a moment to respond.

Grandma looked at Samy as only a grandmother can, and with a great deal of love in her eyes said, "I think you have a great plan and it sounds really interesting. Do you have everything you need?" She smiled and not only gave her stamp of approval, but also offered to help in any way she could.

"Thanks Grandma, you are really going to love it."

Samy looked toward me and then to Grandma. His broad smile and deep dimples alone would have made it impossible to say no to him ... at least from Grandma's perspective.

Grandma who was still staring at her grandson with a look of amazement, pride, and love on her face said, "There is one catch, Grandma wants a big hug and a kiss." Samy quickly obliged.

> *"The greatest danger for most of us is not that we aim too high and we miss, but that we aim too low and we reach it"*
>
> MICHELANGELO

CHAPTER 3

Creativity and Imagination

Grandma insisted that we stay in the kitchen while she made lunch for us. Throughout lunch, Samy described in detail how we had measured the room, planned our layout, and elaborated again, what our plans were. He proudly displayed the list we had made detailing each aspect of our layout!

We finished our lunch and quickly returned upstairs to discuss the next step to making our dream a reality. Now that we had measured the room and received Grandma's endorsement, it was time for us to determine exactly what size to make our train table. We decided that 10 feet by 6 feet surface would give us more than enough room to include all of the features we wanted. All we had to do next was build it! I was impressed with Samy's ability to convert inches into feet and his ability to understand the limitations placed on us by the turning radius of the track we had selected.

We made quite a few sketches of our table to get a better idea of how it would look in the room. When we were satisfied with the size, we moved on to the next phase of our project. Samy had definite ideas about the size of the trains he wanted for our layout, so we directed our attention to track selection. "I never thought there were so many different types of track," Samy said as we looked at the selection on the computer. "We probably should get the same kind I have for my Polar Express," he added.

"Did you know that these tracks are made by the same people who made "Old Bob" 60 years ago Samy?"

"Than this track should last at least 60 years or even more if we take good care of them. Do you think so Grandpa?"

"At least 60 years and you will be able to show it to your grandson," I replied. There was a lot of truth to what I had just said and I knew that just as we were now sharing something that had become a "multi-generational" hobby, it was quite possible that some-day he could be sharing it with his son, grandson, or both. We did not know it, but the journey we were beginning together would become much more than a hobby.

We were sitting at the computer with several different track plans in front of us. One of these looked particularly attractive because it would allow us to include just about all of the things we wanted on our layout.

"Grandpa this won't work unless we make the table bigger," Samy said. I looked closely and sure enough, he was right!

"What makes you think it won't work?" I asked.

"If the track has to be 3 feet apart and we have one inside the other, than we better measure again because it's too close to the edge and the trains could fall off," Samy said dramatically. He may have been only six years old but he had determined that the track plan we were so excited about might not work! We measured again by laying out the tape measure and sure enough not only would our trains be dangerously close to falling off the edge, but we wouldn't have room for certain other features of our layout.

The search for our track plan continued and we finally found one that looked great and would accommodate everything we wanted on our layout. It had two large ovals inside one another and the inner oval would go under the outer at two points giving us the ability to have one train passing under the other. As an added bonus, if we put the appropriate switches in, we could go from inside to the larger outside track! The excitement was building and we were now feeling as though we had accomplished more than look at the magnificent layouts built by teams of people with decades of experience. We printed out two copies of our track plan and taped one to the wall where our layout would hopefully soon be.

"What do you think we should do next?" I said as I turned and looked at my partner.

"I think we can start to build the table today."

"There's only one problem with that, Samy."

"What's that, Grandpa?" Samy said looking somewhat concerned.

"We need a considerable amount of materials such as plywood, two by four lumber, and screws. We can make a list along with a diagram for Dad and talk to him when he gets home from work."

"Good idea, Grandpa, Daddy can build anything," Samy replied confidently.

That night we talked with Dad and Samy told him about the plans for the table and the track plan we found. It was decided that the very first day he could, we would all go to pick up the necessary materials and build the table.

If there was a basement in the house, I was sure that we probably would have considered it for our layout's new home. At this point in time, we had no way of knowing just how much company "Old Bob" would eventually have.

§

The next couple of weeks found us talking about trains, trains and more trains. This is when we discovered eBay, the world's largest concentration of trains, tracks and accessories. After two weeks we had more questions than answers. Should we be looking at O, HO, N, or Z gauge trains? Since "Old Bob" was a Lionel "O" gauge and we had visited a local hobby shop to compare, Samy wanted to stay with the larger gauge train. He already had a Lionel O gauge Polar Express train set that he set up around the Christmas tree each year. This was another reason we decided to stay with the larger O gauge trains.

After spending a considerable amount of time on eBay and various other sites, the questions still outnumbered the answers. It would have been simple if we were looking for something to circle the Christmas tree each year, but we had made the decision to make a layout with a village, train station, mountains, trees, scenery and a train yard! Were we confused at this point? Let's just say we had specific ideas for our layout in mind and were amazed at the number of choices. Samy and I had a time frame for completion that both of us were beginning to doubt.

Only our collective excitement and enthusiasm for our project together, kept us "on track." We wanted to have our layout completed by Christmas which was only two months away! As it turned out, we were in for a big surprise! Very big!

We realized that the amount of choices and opinions we found on the internet might easily overwhelm someone. It was at this time we committed ourselves to focus on the journey, not the destination. I wanted Samy to profit from the time spent with someone you love, not just create a train layout. I also wanted to increase my grandson's knowledge and appreciation of the history of the railroad and the effect it had on people's lives.

§

There definitely was a pattern developing when it came to Samy's choice of trains. He seemed to favor early twentieth century steam engines and the early diesel engines. The layouts he seemed to gravitate to were the ones that featured the villages and architecture of the late nineteenth century to mid twentieth century. He commented many times when we came across an early Victorian home that had very ornate and unique architectural details seldom seen in houses today.

"Do you know what is missing on almost all of the train layouts we have looked at so far Grandpa? Without waiting for an answer he said, mountains!"

"Maybe it's because it is easier to build elevated track and put some scenery behind it so it 'looks' like a mountain or use murals on the walls adjacent to the train layout. Your observation is a good one Samy, and I would be willing to bet that if you type in a search for model railroad mountains it would not yield many results."

We did just that and the very few results we came up with were some very poorly made paper mache attempts at making a mountain. The prices on them were astronomical when you considered what you were paying for. They were small and not very realistic. Samy looked at one in particular and said, "That looks like a growth that should be removed!" I agreed as we both laughed. The way that Samy expresses himself constantly amazes. We were still laughing at what we had named "Growth Mountain" when Samy asked, "Are we going to build a mountain on our layout?"

I held my hands in the air as high as possible and said, "This is how high our mountain is going to be. We will build it right through the roof so you can see the peak from the outside!"

"OH Grandpa...I want a big mountain but I think it's your idea that is through the roof."

"Perhaps you are right, and this is one idea that I don't think our planning board will approve." I then conceded that my idea was a little bit "over the top."

We both had a great time searching for models and tunnels on the internet. We marveled at how unrealistic and toy-like what we were seeing was. Do people really buy these? We concluded that if you did not have or use your imagination you might be tempted to buy one.

"I would much rather build something than buy it!" Samy said this with a glow of enthusiasm and his characteristic sense of wonder. This is a concept we should encourage by creating opportunities for our children.

In that regard, we were in complete agreement. Samy's "build it vs. buy it" theory was a good one and had a great deal of merit. He did add that there are certain things such as the engine, track, and some accessories we would have to buy.

"There are some things in our lives that you simply cannot buy with any amount of money. These are the most important things that we often take for granted," I said to my grandson. This was something I knew Samy fully understood.

It was clear that if we were going to achieve the results we wanted it would be necessary for us to create much of our layout ourselves. Samy was not only aware of this, but also looked forward to it. "I think it's going to be fun to build all these things like the mountain, tunnels, and maybe even a bridge. Do you think we can finish them all?" Samy had questions about the somewhat aggressive plans we had, but wanted to complete them all.

"Absolutely, I answered. I think we might have to adjust our target date for completing our layout by a few months at the very least." This moment, at least in my mind, was when our journey had officially begun. The look on Samy's face was one of determination and excitement and he could not wait to begin what we would refer to as our journey together. We still had no idea what was in store for us or where our project would lead us.

Samy and I were only just beginning an exciting adventure together. We were still in the "planning stage." We had no idea how much fun it was going to be, how long it would take, or how elaborate it would become. Certainly, we did not know it would become a "time machine" allowing us insights far into the past and future as well. I sensed that Samy possessed certain abilities that relied on imagination not rote memorization of facts and an appreciation for circumstances and things that affected people's lives. His strong moral code and underlying strength of character made this six year-old exceptional.

§

Our project was indeed "open-ended" and we were comfortable with the fact that each day we seem to add something to it. We were also happy that the new challenges that we faced very often, presented us with opportunities to find creative solutions. Most of these solutions involved working together on something you could not buy such as our mountain. The only thing that we agreed was constant was that we were never quite sure what the future had in store for us. Change itself was the constant and we welcomed it with much enthusiasm.

Discussing a target date for completion was something we did quite often. We wanted to set goals for ourselves that were attainable. Our own plans became more elaborate and required revision of these goals on a regular basis.

There are many people who have let pessimism replace their passion for making our world a better place. Samy agreed that there is nothing we could not overcome. Samy summed it up best when he said to me, "This might look hard to do but we will come up with a way to do it, it may just take us a little longer."

"That's where our patience and perseverance come in to play," I added.

Samy smiled and said, "Don't forget our creativity and imagination."

My answer to those who look to the future with overwhelming pessimism, and those who say things will never be as good in this world as they once were is a simple one. The answer is in the twinkle in my grandson's eye, his infectious sense of wonder, his extraordinary common sense, and phenomenal character! The world is a much better place because Samy is in it.

"Whoever teaches his son teaches not alone his son but also his son's son and so on to the end of generations"

HEBREW PROVERB

CHAPTER 4

Three Generations

The telephone rang and when I picked it up, the unmistakable and excited voice of my archeological partner was on the other end. He was extremely excited and said "Grandpa, Daddy said if you want to go pick up the supplies for the train table he will help us build it today."

"Great buddy, what time did you have in mind?"

"Right now," he said enthusiastically and without any hesitation. "We'll pick you up and go to the store."

"I'll be waiting for you." I responded, almost laughing that he had given me so much advanced notice.

"Thanks Grandpa, I'll see you in a few minutes."

At that moment, I was congratulating myself for moving the assortment of furniture out of what was to be our train room when I heard the doorbell ring. Samy and his father were at the door. I called down to them and Samy said excitedly "Grandpa, are you upstairs?"

"Yes, I have a wall stretcher and I'm trying to make the room bigger for an even larger train table."

"Oh Grandpa..."

I turned to come downstairs and before I knew it, there was my grandson in front of me presumably to make sure I was coming right down. I held my hand out, Samy slapped me "five", and I asked, "Are you excited Samy? I know I am."

"Very excited Grandpa, and Daddy said he has some great ideas for the train table."

"I knew he would. We have our carpenter today and I'm sure by today's end we will have our table."

"This is going to be so cool," Samy replied with a combination of excitement and enthusiasm in his voice.

"You bet it is, especially with Daddy's help, we will have a professionally made train table."

"Can we put the track on today?" Samy asked excitedly.

"Let's see how far we get with the table and then we can start laying down the track."

§

Samy has always been a bright, energetic child, who possesses more patience than I remember having had as a child. He is grateful for those things he is given, and quick to thank you when appropriate. There is no doubt that his parents are responsible for this. Today was no different. At the moment, he was surrounded by his father and grandfather on the way to purchase supplies for his soon to be train table. As the pickup truck pulled into the parking lot of the store, the excitement of sharing this moment changed this experience into something much more than building a train table. These are the moments in time that we should cherish, since they create memories that we will remember with our children for the rest of our lives.

As we pulled in to the massive parking lot of one of the area's home improvement stores I quickly estimated it was at least a half mile from the beginning of the parking lot to the entrance of the store. We parked closest to the "building supplies" entrance where small mountains of exterior lumber were neatly stacked. Adjacent to the side of the store on the left perimeter of the lot were rows of garden sheds that stood like a small village.

Together we exited the truck and went through the large automatic doors. This was the kind of outlet that has become the primary source of materials for homeowners and contractors throughout the country. The scope and size of these stores has grown tremendously in the past few decades. These stores certainly did not exist back in "Old Bob's" day. Did we ever think we would need a GPS device to locate the nails we needed? We are now measuring the size of some of these superstores with fractions of a mile, not to mention the phenomenal height of the interior.

§

Samy was no stranger to this type of store and was accustomed to shopping here quite often with his parents. I wondered what it would be like to experience the massive size of one these stores through the eyes of a six-year-old. Samy held on to the list and followed his father to the Lumber department, while I looked for one of those large carts for the two by fours and plywood. After finding one of the carts distributed throughout the lumber aisles, I walked through the neatly stacked piles of lumber and caught up with the rest of the crew near the plywood. We picked out the sheets of plywood we needed and headed toward the two by four lumber. The two by fours would make the frame and legs of our layout. Samy was a great help in choosing only those that were straight for our train table. Samy, Dad, and Grandpa agreed that only the best would do. We agreed to let Dad do the rest of the heavy lifting and Samy and I headed for the hardware department to pick up the rest of the supplies on our list.

We found one of the smaller carts and were on our way to the hardware aisles. Our destination was the equivalent of running halfway down a football field and we were rapidly approaching the fifty yard line. The various screws were stacked by size, weight, length, and usage. There were literally thousands of boxes to choose from stretching down an aisle that seemed endless. After finding the woods screws we needed, we placed them in our cart and began to head back toward the "goal line", where Dad was waiting for us to check out.

§

Samy's look of determination was turning into one of satisfaction and excitement at the prospect of our train table becoming a reality. Surely, most of our work would be done today! Neither of us realized what the weeks and months ahead had in store for us. We did realize however that a simple trip to the home improvement store was more than a routine trip to pick up supplies. It became one of the first legs of our journey and created memories seldom associated with a home improvement store.

"What do you think, Sam, did we get everything on our list?" We read the list together and were satisfied we had everything we needed.

"We sure did Grandpa, especially those extra boxes of screws." He was referring to the boxes I had put in the cart at the last minute to make sure we did not run short.

"You mean my insurance screws?"

"Yes Grandpa..."

"Sam, set a course for the checkout line warp factor 6"

"The course is set, Grandpa"

"Do you have Daddy in visual range?"

"Yes I do, Grandpa."

When we reached the checkout line Sam noticed a few extra larger pieces of lumber on the lumber cart and asked his dad what they were. Before he could answer Sam said, "They wouldn't by any chance be insurance lumber, Dad?"

"Insurance lumber, what is that?" Dad asked.

"It's extra to make sure you don't run out."

"No, they are not extra, but these pieces will be a frame for the outside of the table."

"Leave it to your father Samy, you were right we did choose the right contractor!"

"We sure did, Grandpa this is going to be better than the tables we saw on the computer!"

§

I reminded myself of the days I pushed Samy
stores such as these in a stroller. How was it poss
I had not grown older but Samy did? Wasn't it just yesterday that Grandma and Grandpa were shopping for Samy
at "Babies R Us?"

We checked out, pushed our carts through the large
automatic doors, and headed for the pickup truck.
After loading our supplies we headed for home and
the future home of our new train table. We watched as
the size of the home improvement store decreased as we
pulled out of the parking lot. It seemed the smaller the
store became, the greater our enthusiasm for our project
became.

It was not just picking up supplies that made this
otherwise routine trip special. Grandpa, Dad, and
Samy represented three generations in the truck that
day. Three generations working together to create
memories that would surely never be forgotten. Only
time would tell just how significant these memories
would be for each of them. We all knew that our journey would have an impact on each of us as well as the
strong possibility that a fourth generation would be
affected by what we did here today. This was something that had generated many discussions about the
past, present, and future!

§

There is no doubt that we were both fascinated by the subject of "time". We had often joked about the building of a time machine or a time capsule and both subjects had led to some very interesting discussions. Temporal mechanics, we agreed was a subject that could give anyone a headache. We wanted to build something that was special, but we did not know just how interesting our journey would become. At this point, we could only "imagine" where our journey would take us. The sense of mystery and adventure we associated with our journey was extremely appealing to both of us. Although we had put our time machine on hold temporarily, we referred to it often. The plans for the "flux capacitor" were still in the research and development stage. The plutonium-powered DeLorean ... well that was another story!

We knew that the memories we create on occasions such as this would last a lifetime. These are the "snapshots in time" we hold so dear. We hoped that they would serve as a basis for the next generation to create more memories of their own. We vowed to do our best to make that happen. This is the reason that one generation should stand on the shoulders of the one preceding it. It makes possible that which we previously thought was not.

§

I could not help but remember that the hands that were holding two by four lumber, were those that belonged to an infant, who not that long ago, clasped his tiny hand around my finger for the first time, and changed my life forever!

"The four cornerstones of character on which the structure of this nation was built are: Initiative, Imagination, Individuality, and Independence"

EDDIE RICKENBACKER

CHAPTER 5

Is it Really Happening?

The truck backed into the driveway and we immediately began to unload the material we had picked up for our train table. Samy and I placed it on the driveway according to size and Dad went home to pick up the tools he needed. My grandson and I stood in the driveway looking at the substantial amount of building materials.

"Grandpa, have you ever built a train table?"

"No Sam but with your Dad here it shouldn't be difficult at all."

"So this is your first train table too."

"Yes it is, Sam, and I am as excited as you are."

It was a cool December day and we really hadn't noticed just how much the temperature had dropped. We went into the house where Grandma suggested we both have some hot chocolate. As we sat talking about our project and how it was finally taking shape, Samy suggested that we make a list of all of those things we wanted to put on our train layout. It wasn't long before we heard the truck backing into the driveway and both of us went out to greet Dad.

Dad suggested that it would be a good idea to do all the cutting outside and Samy and I could take the pieces upstairs for final assembly. He set up his table saw in the driveway and went to work. I knew it would have taken me three times as long to complete our table not to mention how much better the result was going to be. We were fortunate that Dad was able to help us with the construction. The sound of the saw cutting through the plywood sheets was music to our ears. The smell of the freshly cut lumber brought back memories of something new and exciting. Each cut brought us closer to our train table and into the fascinating world of model railroading. Our journey was indeed just beginning.

"Grandpa these are like puzzle pieces," Samy said as we pulled each completed piece into the garage and eagerly awaited the creation of the next rare work of art. They were pieces to a much bigger puzzle and the completed puzzle was something we only dreamed about until today. We now know there will be a time to look back and remember the significance of what we were doing here today!

When there were a sufficient number of pieces, we began to take them upstairs and laid them out for final assembly. We waited for our "contractor" to arrive upstairs to supervise the construction. The process of building our table began after we were sure that we had all the pieces to this giant puzzle.

The frame that would hold the surface of our table started to take shape. One by one, each piece that had previously been just a pile of lumber now looked like a work of art to both of us. We securely screwed the surface of the table in place. Samy drilled pilot holes and I followed up with screws in the places that Dad marked. Before we knew it, an hour had passed and the tabletop and frame were complete. All that remained were the legs in each corner and additional legs strategically placed near the center. After fastening the additional supports to the table, we remarked how the table could now hold our combined weight with ease. We complimented ourselves on having the precision of a NASCAR pit crew and then stood back to admire our creation.

We did realize that most of the credit and the work belonged to Dad. Samy was the first to thank his father and tell him how much he appreciated the train table. After all, Dad had made the precise cuts and measurements without which our table would not have turned out so well.

§

The moment had arrived and we were looking at what we could previously only visualize. We would create our very own work of art on this blank canvas. Samy was clearly impressed with the sheer size of the table and said "Wow! We could fit five trains on this with a village, a mountain, tunnels and more."

"Can you see it Samy?"

"I sure can, Grandpa" Samy replied without the least bit of hesitation.

"What do you see?"

"I see mountains, villages, track, "Old Bob", tunnels, and a train yard."

"You know there is no limit to your imagination, Samy and it seems you just added a few things to our list."

"Just a few Grandpa" Samy replied grinning from ear to ear.

"Let's help put all the tools away and clean up before we begin phase two. What do you think?"

"Great idea, Grandpa, this table is so cool!" Samy said genuinely excited.

Samy thanked his dad for building the train table for us and gave him a big hug before he left for work.

About an hour later, we had finished putting all the tools away. We decided that vacuuming the room and the surface of the table was a good idea. Samy vacuumed every square inch of the tabletop with the shop vacuum.

"Sam, this is quite possibly the strongest train table in existence."

"It sure is Grandpa and it looks so big."

§

"Do you remember when we were sitting in the big closet and talking about our secret clubhouse for members only?"

"You mean the very first day when we discovered 'Old Bob'?"

Samy crawled under the fortress we had just built and began to move around under it. He had just made a discovery he couldn't wait to share. Samy went on to explain what he had discovered and how we could close in the front side with something and no one would know if anyone was under our bunker. He invited me under and after securing a couple of throw pillows, the two of us were sitting in our new clubhouse. The fact that the three walls of the room enclosed us did make it seem like we had created a room and another meeting place. As I crawled out of our new structure, Samy asked where I was going and I told him to wait right there.

I came back with a couple of markers and said, "This is for years from now when someone looks under the table they can see who constructed it and whose project it was."

"You mean like a sort of time capsule, Grandpa?"

"You're exactly right, I read a story about these kids who decided to make a time capsule and bury it for 15 years. They all agreed to open it together on the same day they buried it only 15 years later."

Do you remember what they put in it?" Samy asked.

"They all put pictures of themselves and their families in it and a picture of all of them together. They made a list of all of the things that were going on in the world and put newspaper articles in it as well. They even put in a flash drive that had a lot of other things on it."

"This story sounds like a really good one; do you remember how old they were?" Samy responded enthusiastically.

"They were thirteen years old when they buried it, but the story ended long before they opened it. That was the only part they should have left in the story."

"Maybe the author of the story wanted you to use your imagination to figure out how each of them turned out."

When we were finished writing, the words "Sam and Grandpa December 2010" were written across one of the center beams. We talked about how buildings often had a cornerstone with the year they were built inscribed on them. This was our cornerstone and we were quite impressed with our work. This also was to become our time capsule we would leave for future generations to open.

Perhaps years from now Samy would show his son or daughter the "cornerstone" of our train table and explain how at this point our incredible journey was just beginning!

Samy thought this was a fantastic idea and suggested that we write our names and the date on one of the legs as well. Samy looked over at me and said, "It's too bad you didn't write your name and your dad's name on the box we found 'Old Bob' in."

"I would have liked that Samy, I really would."

"At least you have all those photo albums with pictures when you were young," Samy said in a way that gave me the feeling he was trying to console me for not having my name or my father's name on the box. The thoughtfulness I had come to expect from my grandson was remarkable and something I did not take for granted.

"You are right Samy and they are something every family should have. They are the history of a family in pictures." Samy along with his mother and father enjoyed looking through these albums and did so quite frequently.

Samy had a keen sense for stories about when his parents were young and relied on me as his number one resource. He had an insatiable appetite for any stories that happened before he was born and I was more than willing to supply him with all he wanted to hear. I knew that there might come a day when Samy was not quite as "enthusiastic" about my story-telling. Until that day came, and I hoped it never would, I enjoyed it immensely when Samy would ask me to tell a story.

We had shifted from hearing stories about the past to a combination of these stories and making memories of our own. Samy and I were on a journey together that would create memories. These are the "snapshots in time" that would remain in our hearts forever.

"The pessimist sees difficulty in every opportunity. The optimist sees the opportunity in every difficulty"

WINSTON CHURCHILL

CHAPTER 6

Patience and Perseverance

We found our research into every facet of the history and the building of the railroads fascinating. This was perhaps another motivating force that led us to embrace model railroading as a key component of our journey. We were enjoying it immensely and that was not likely to change in the near future. Over the course of the first few months Samy had read several books on the great railroads and how they changed America. We had been on hundreds of web sites together and felt as though we had seen everything there was to see about model railroading. We learned how the railroads affected the way people lived, worked, and played. Our continuing efforts opened up more possibilities that we had not dreamed of when we saw "Old Bob" for the first time.

The educational opportunities our journey presented us with seemed almost limitless. The enthusiasm Samy displayed was the key we were given to unlock countless new doors into a world of exciting learning opportunities. Together we were determined to take advantage of them all.

§

Today, on the screen in front of us was an engine Samy had seen in one of the many books he had borrowed from the library. We had not seen a model of it until now. This Milwaukee diesel engine was extremely detailed. Its iconic colors made it instantly recognizable and the design was breathtaking.

"Grandpa this is the one I told you about. This is the one that was in the book with the big pictures of all of the train engines! Do you remember it? We looked at it about a week ago."

"Do I remember it? You bet I do! This was in the book that had the really great photographs and information about each engine and the rail line it serviced."

Seeing it blown up in full color on a 24-inch screen, added to the already impressive characteristics the image on the screen possessed. The top and approximately 25%

of the sides were black interrupted by bright orange that extended down to the walk that circled the engine. The rails were black and contrasted nicely against the orange sides. The remainder of the engine and wheels were also black.

"I can't believe we found it! This is so cool! Look at the details on this, the rails, the lights and it has twelve wheels! This looks so real!"

"Sam, I'm getting the impression that you like it."

"Like it... I love this engine. Look at the number on the side. I even think it's the same one that's in the book."

"You're right Sam, this is one of the most detailed we have seen and we have seen a lot in the past month."

"This would look so great on our layout and could be our first diesel to haul logs and stuff up the mountain."

To say my grandson was excited would be the greatest understatement of the century. The truth is we both were. We must have looked at that engine for at least an hour that day before Samy came up with his plan for getting the Milwaukee on our layout. It was early in December and Samy was making his list for Santa. He looked at me wide-eyed and with a confidence that only someone with a sure-fire plan has and said, "Grandpa, I know what I am going to do. I'll ask Santa for the Milwaukee for our train layout."

"That certainly sounds like a plan to me." I replied in agreement with Samy's plan noting that Christmas was not far away.

§

This engine was an exact replica of one of the most iconic engines to ever to grace the tracks anywhere. The Milwaukee diesel in front of us by its very design exhibited the strength that enabled it to pull large loads and traverse mountain passes that early steam engines had difficulty with. This Milwaukee engine and its predecessors performed this task effortlessly.

Closer examination revealed an illuminated cabin, operating lights in front, grab railing all the way around the engine, horns on top, and a bell. There were also extremely life-like windows in the cab and if you closed your eyes, you could easily imagine the engineer inside. Fortunately, there were many photographs taken from different angles and we were able to view and enlarge them all. Little did either of us know that we would be doing this again, many times!

The pictures we were viewing were on eBay. The price, which of course was not an issue since Santa was now bringing it, was also displayed. I did see it was an "auction" type format, which means people place bids on an item for a specified length of time and the item goes to the highest bidder.

I was confident that Santa would have no problem with that or he may have another supplier. Either way time was growing short and the pressure was mounting.

Our Milwaukee diesel engine needed cars to pull so as we looked on eBay and a few of our favorite other train sites. We wanted to find cars the Milwaukee engine would have pulled. We found a boxcar, flatcar, automobile carrier and the perfect matching caboose.

§

Two weeks later we were on the computer when Samy turned to me and said, "Grandpa let's go to that place on eBay and look at the Milwaukee diesel engine again."

We typed in the search box "Milwaukee diesel engine" and sure enough, there was our tremendous Milwaukee engine. This time the picture had the word "sold" across it. Samy noticed it immediately.

"Does this mean we can't get it?" Samy said sounding somewhat disappointed.

"What it means is that on this particular site someone purchased it."

"Did somebody buy it?" Samy asked again.

"Someone could have, but there are other possibilities."

"If no one else bought it then why would it say sold on it?"

"Samy, this is not the only place to buy trains, and if anyone can get this engine, Santa can! Right now I think we should look at more track."

We typed in a search for the type of track we needed although I could see that my grandson's mind was elsewhere. The possibility that the Milwaukee engine was "sold", especially in the eyes of a six year old, was extremely disappointing.

"Grandpa, I know this is not the only site that sells trains, but we weren't able to see it anywhere else when we searched for it."

"Remember what Mom always tells you to have."

"I know we should all have patience and perseverance," Samy said somewhat concerned about his Milwaukee engine.

"Let's get going on the track or we won't have anything for our train to run on." We looked at the track pieces we needed and put our order together. Our layout was now going to have four switches which would allow us to have a train switch from the inner track to the outer. Things were moving along nicely and we were getting more things accomplished every week.

"There are two types of switches that you can buy. The first type is a 'manual' switch that the user has to physically turn so the train goes in the direction you want. The second type of switch is a 'remote' switch, that has a wire attached so you can operate it from anywhere on the layout with the push of a button. We would probably put this type of switch controller next to our transformers and switches in our control panel."

"I like the manual switches better because we have to switch them instead of pushing a button," Samy said wasting no time expressing his preference for manual switches instead of remote switches.

"Remember, if you have a manual switch on the far end of your layout you have to get up and switch it manually. The remote allows you to push a button from our control center."

"Really, Grandpa, how hard is it to get up and walk to the other side of the table?" Samy said expressing a definite preference for manual switches.

"Not hard at all, I wanted to make sure you knew the difference between the two types of switches. Did you know the remote switches are two and one half times the price of the manual switches? This way you get what you want and we save money in the process that we can spend somewhere else. Remember, you are the chief architect on this project."

We ordered the necessary track and switches that day and in spite of our Milwaukee problem, everything was going quite smoothly. The mere "bumps in the road" we encountered, Samy agreed, that through our patience, perseverance and creativity we would conquer them all.

§

"The switches we ordered are going to be really cool." Samy said excitedly. He had always opted for toys you had to push instead of batteries and enjoyed playing with his cars for hours. He told me once that he liked it that way because he could create situations where his cars would go where only he wanted them to. We proudly taped our track plan to the front edge of our new table and tried our hardest to think of a way we could get one oval of track to pass over the other. This was the greatest obstacle we had to overcome. Samy and I agreed that so far it had been a lot of fun experimenting with potential solutions and that we would not give up!

"We probably should do more research on this and leave it for another day."

"You have to have patience and perseverance, Grandpa!"

"You are absolutely right Samy; we will accomplish our goals one way or another. Have you ever heard the expression 'It's always darkest before the dawn'?"

"I think I have but what does it mean?"

"At dawn the sun comes up and everything is bright. Before that it's dark."

"I get it when the sun comes up you can see clearly, but before that you are in the dark," Samy replied quite proud of himself.

"Excellent. I could not have said it better myself, however I could sing it if you want me to."

"Sing what?" Samy asked, somewhat confused at his grandfather's offer to sing something.

"Do you remember when I used to sing 'The sun will come out tomorrow'?"

Samy just shook his head. I could only guess what my grandson was thinking. Was it "I was two years old then, now I'm almost seven. I love you but please don't sing."

It was at that moment that Samy looked at me excitedly and said he might know what happened to the Milwaukee engine. He clearly had not stopped thinking about the possibility of not getting the Milwaukee engine. I knew how much Samy loved this engine. He had talked about it quite often and even done some research of his own at the library. Samy had requested that we look for it online on many occasions. He even brought home a book from the library that had pictures of it along with its history. Today he felt that this legendary engine slipped from his grasp.

"I think I know why it says 'sold' on the Milwaukee engine. It's because of Santa!" Samy exclaimed with a combination of pure joy and pride in in his voice at having solved the mystery that was plaguing him since he saw the sold sign across the Milwaukee.

"You may be right Sam, you just may be right. We should have thought of that! Since we were looking at one of the largest selections of trains anywhere, Santa probably uses them to fill some of his orders for Christmas."

Samy's eyes grew wider, his smile broadened and his dimples became deeper as he said, "That is exactly what I was thinking!"

I have seen one of what I now call "Samy's light bulb moments" before, and each one is better than the one before it. They are not just an intellectual experience but a physical one as well. His eyes, smile, dimples, and his voice combine to make the expression of a thought or idea a memorable experience. This was one of those "snapshots in time" that we will long remember. I want to be there always to share these memories with him.

§

The magic of Christmas, a six year old's sense of wonder, and my love for my grandson came together that very moment to remind me, that you are only six once!

"If you can dream it, you can do it"

Walt Disney

CHAPTER 7

Dreams Do Come True

The weeks leading up to Christmas had Samy think-ing more about the Milwaukee engine. He expressed concern that the beautiful Milwaukee diesel engine he had seen on the internet may have been sold. He reached the conclusion that Santa had purchased the Milwaukee engine and that he should not worry about it. After all, he is Santa Claus!

He would ask Santa when he saw him in person. Santa had never let him down before and he was sure he would not do so this year. On the other hand, was he sure? I had assured him he would find out Christmas morning and that anticipation is half the fun.

This year we were going to a magnificent estate located approximately forty minutes from home to see Santa. Our destination was located on four hundred acres of prime rolling meadows, woodlands, and lakefront property. This was part of an estate left by a retired textile executive who wanted a world-class botanical garden constructed and developed on this site for all to enjoy.

It was on this estate that Santa would listen to all boys and girls who wished to come and present him with their Christmas list. Samy was extremely excited this year and could not wait to see Santa. He had made his list and emailed it to Santa but there was nothing like delivering it to Santa in person. The Milwaukee engine was on the top of Samy's list this year and he was looking forward to Christmas morning.

"Grandpa, will Santa have his reindeer with him where we are going?" Samy asked.

"This is a huge estate with a lot of woodlands and meadows so there is plenty of room for reindeer. I don't know if we will see them but I suppose it wouldn't hurt to ask Santa."

"I wonder if they have trains there. That would be so cool and we could get some ideas from it."

"This is the first time we have been there so I am not sure exactly what we are going to see. All the information we have gathered describes it as a beautiful place to visit and I am sure that is the reason Santa chose it as well."

§

Tens of thousands of twinkling Christmas lights decorated the entrance to the property. The long, winding road, lined with expertly decorated trees, guided visitors to the main building. There were decorations as far as the eye could see. In the distance we could see a very well lit building. Surely, this is where Santa was. Mom, Dad, Grandma, Grandpa and Samy were making what would become their traditional trip to these beautifully decorated gardens to see Santa.

The visitor's pavilion had a grand entrance decorated with several evergreen trees, and some that were made entirely out of orchids. We looked to see where Santa was located and found a room with a massive Christmas tree lavishly decorated and almost touching the thirty foot high ceiling. Beautifully wrapped presents adorned the base of the tree. There was a very large fireplace with a fire burning and a large red chair to its right which was obviously reserved for the guest of honor. Since Santa had not yet arrived, we went in to the main room to wait and have some hot chocolate.

To the right of the large main room was a smaller room with a train layout depicting a winter scene, village, and snow covered mountains. Instantly, we found ourselves standing next to the display admiring the trains, mountains, and tunnels. Samy was completely engrossed and excited with each pass the little train made as it entered and exited the tunnels under the snow-capped mountains.

The illuminated houses that were nestled in the small village gave it a very life-like appearance. "Grandpa, do you think we could build a mountain like this and have tunnels through it something like this one has?"

"I don't see why not Sam, only ours will have to be quite a bit larger since our trains will be three times as large."

"Could we make a village with stores, a school and a church?" Samy asked.

"Anything is possible if you put your mind to it."

"Let's start with the mountain and do the others after we finish the mountain," Samy said enthusiastically and with a great deal of resolve in his voice.

"That will have to be a big mountain. It will have to be very big if we want to remain true to scale."

Making or drawing objects to scale is a concept that many people find difficult to grasp. Samy had displayed an aptitude for scale in our early drawings and recognized the need to maintain the scale throughout our project. Perhaps his desire to become an architect was more than a coincidence. I wanted very much to be there to provide him with opportunities to succeed whatever they might be.

"We could make a whole forest on the side of the mountain like we saw in the pictures in my train book."

Before I was able to respond, Mom told us that Santa had arrived and it was time to go to Santa's room. We made sure our cameras were ready and followed Mom to see Santa.

§

As we approached Santa's room, we saw him through the open French doors. There was the jolly old man dressed in his deep red suit trimmed in white with a wide black belt. His white hair and beard flowed majestically from his face and his spectacles were perched just low enough to allow him to see over them. Shiny black boots contrasted with his red cap and matched his belt perfectly. We saw him sit down in his chair in anticipation of receiving his young guests, in a remarkably similar way a king would receive his subjects. Today Santa would listen to requests from all children regarding their wishes for Christmas. Today he was royalty to those who would come to him and make their wishes known.

We waited patiently and when the time came, Samy approached him and we heard Santa say "Merry Christmas"

"Merry Christmas Santa," Samy answered.

We took as many pictures as we could and both Santa and Samy were a photographer's dream. Samy came back to where we were standing with a huge smile and look of satisfaction on his face.

I knew what was on the top of Samy's list this year however, at that moment only Samy and Santa knew exactly what the topic of their conversation was. Samy was more than willing to share his conversation with Santa with us. His mother and father asked him about his conversation with Santa and Samy said, "Santa is so nice. He asked me what I wanted for Christmas and I told him about all the things I wanted and how we sent him a list."

"What was the first thing on your list?" his mother asked.

"I think Grandpa knows what that is."

As we left the hallway leading to Santa's room, we noticed another room with a great deal of activity. There were five long tables set up and each was more beautiful than the one before it. Behind each table sat at least a half dozen people who were there to assist any boy or girl who wanted to participate in the various arts and craft activities. If you chose to participate, you could decorate pinecones, Christmas balls, evergreen branches, and all sorts of things. Paste and glue was readily available to dip your project in and decorate.

I took pictures of Samy decorating his pinecone and even decorated one myself. This was truly a very magical place to spend an evening especially during the Christmas season.

"Can we go outside now and see all the lights?" Samy asked excitedly.

"We sure can," his mother answered as she took his hand and led us through the magnificent doors that led to the outside. There was Christmas music playing throughout the entire estate. The walkways that led visitors through the exquisitely decorated gardens were bustling with people. I could not help but notice how happy they all looked, as I thought about what a joyous time of year this was.

Samy led us tirelessly through these magical gardens, as he marveled at how everything was so intricately decorated. He stopped in front of what appeared to be a sixty-foot high tree that had thousands of lights and illuminated balls that were at least twelve inches in diameter and said, "Grandpa do you think we could decorate the trees in front of our house like this?"

"We would probably need a fire truck or one of those 'cherry pickers' that tree cutters use. I suppose we could do it if we could persuade Dad to go up that high on a ladder." I answered.

Samy laughed and said, "You are probably right. That would be a little bit too high for our ladder."

There is and always has been something special about seeing things through the eyes of a child. Christmas has always magnified all that is good and right with the world especially when viewed this way.

We continued to tour the grounds of this magnificent estate. The entire estate sparkled under the glow of tens of thousands of lights. There were colored spotlights that shined through the fountains of water that cascaded down over steps creating mini waterfalls for a distance of fifty yards or more. Walkways on both sides of this spectacular water feature were lined with a variety of different shrubs and were also trimmed with lights and decorations. The larger trees were adorned with lights and decorations proportional to their size. Domes of lights were constructed in such a way that you could stand under them, and the arches that graced the walkways twinkled with light as you walked on the pathways beneath them.

"I can't believe how many lights they put on the trees!" It was clear that Samy was having a great time. He did not want to miss anything and commented on everything. He was clearly impressed and appreciative of everything he had experienced. The gardens were spectacular and Grandma and I agreed that we had never seen anything like it.

§

Collectively, however, they did not compare with the twinkle in my grandson's eyes!

> *"Character is doing the right thing when nobody is looking"*
>
> J.C. WATTS

CHAPTER 8

Problem or Opportunity?

The next few weeks Samy and I struggled with our track plan. We had found that two by four lumber was the perfect size for our track. It measured three and one-half inches, which was the exact width of our track. Our goal was to gradually increase the incline of the track until one oval was able to pass over the other leaving sufficient room for our train. Sound simple? It was anything but!

We cut pieces of lumber in one-quarter inch increments ranging from one-quarter inch to five inches until we had several pieces of each size. The result was nothing short of comical. We definitely should have made a video and sent it into "America's Funniest Video's Show". We had read about the maximum grade you should require your engine to climb, however we were limited by the size of the layout. The longest "run" we could have was approximately fifteen feet. Keeping in mind the fact that what goes up must come down, we began our "trial and error" method of track design.

Samy and I experimented with several different combinations ranging to the "gentlest" of grades to more severe ones. Each required testing our engine with one of us at the controls, and the other ready to catch our engine as it fell off the track. Initially, Samy would look disappointed at our lack of success and had to be reassured. Two days of "experimenting" and multiple two by fours later, we found ourselves laughing hysterically when a trial run failed. Samy was laughing uncontrollably when he said, "Grandpa, what are we going to do with all of these two by four pieces?" He was pointing at the bags of pieces we had cut and separated into different bags in an effort to remain somewhat scientific about the whole "trial and error" process. I looked down at the bags Samy was pointing to and began laughing. We apparently did not realize just how many were cut and accumulated.

"Are you going to let a small setback like this one discourage you?" I said to my grandson who was still laughing. Admittedly, I had an extremely difficult time holding back the laughter.

"Small setback! Samy exclaimed, the lumber yard is going to run out of two by fours if we keep this up!"

"I think we need to develop Plan B." We both were laughing hysterically by now and realized that it was time to revise our strategy. We agreed that our small "setback" required further thought.

"We need a 'Plan B, C, and D," Samy responded, still laughing.

"All we have to do is..."

Samy was standing on the opposite side of the lay-out and at this point I was interrupted by the sight of Samy holding up two bags of two by four pieces on top of three other large bags he had placed on the table in front of him.

"What were you saying Grandpa?"

The sight of my grandson, almost totally obscured by five huge bags of two by four experimental pieces, was enough to make both of us break into uncontrollable laughter. We both realized that we indeed did need a "Plan B." We may not have been successful in designing one track to pass over the other, but we had created something even more special. We knew that the laughter we shared that day was certainly not a failure, but a priceless memory that would take its place among the "snapshots in time" we created together.

We realized that what we were trying to accomplish by having one oval of track pass over the other required a grade that was much too steep. Our strategy in this regard would have to be changed. Necessity dictated that our layout was going to have two levels! The outer perimeter of track would be elevated to accommodate our mountain and give us the ability to have one train pass over the other. We were enjoying our "setbacks" because they led to our successes, and only enhanced our time together. There was a great deal of laughter especially when we looked at the bags full of wood scraps we had cut to "temporarily" elevate our track. Samy was encouraged by the fact that our new strategy would involve more work and enhance not only our layout, but the time we spent together.

§

"Grandpa, I think our next step should be our mountain."

"Once we agree on the location and height of our mountain, all that we have to do is build it."

"Do you think we will be able to finish the mountain before Christmas?" Samy inquired with a hopeful tone in his voice.

"Do you mean this Christmas or next?" I responded.

We both laughed again as we looked at the bags of scrap lumber that were now under the table. This was lumber we would use to support our second level.

"I think it is time we had another planning board meeting." I suggested.

"I think so too, Grandpa."

We met in our newly constructed conference room where we had a lamp and all the supplies we would use frequently. We sketched out our second level and mountain and discussed how to build it. These are the moments to be thankful for remembering that it is more about the "journey" and less about the "destination."

"What color do we want the mountain to be?" Samy asked.

"I really haven't thought about it, Samy, have you?"

"When I was looking at the pictures in the book I was reading about the early railroads, I saw a lot of mountains that looked almost red."

"There are certain areas of the country where you will find a lot of the red rock that you are talking about. I know you would like a turn of the century American village style, so why don't we try and be as authentic as we can and match both the time period with the area of the country?"

"Maybe it could be the area we live in now or some-where like it," Samy responded without knowing that his grandfather had a plan in mind.

"I have an idea but we'll have to take a walk to show you."

"Where are we going?"Samy asked quizzically not knowing what was coming next.

§

"Get your jacket, take some of those bags, and follow me, we're going on an expedition." I knew Samy loved these spontaneous activities especially if they involved sports or the outdoors. Samy grabbed his jacket and the bags and we were out of the door in minutes. I told him we were going exploring and to think of our expedition as an archaeological adventure. The look on his face told me Samy loved every minute of it and so did I.

"You do realize that we could discover gold or something like that."

"Maybe the fossil remains of a dinosaur." Samy said enthusiastically.

"Very good, Samy, I'm impressed!"

"Mom just took me to the library and one of the books I got was all about dinosaurs."

We were approximately one hundred and fifty yards from the destination we were both looking forward to. I had walked past it many times but today it was truly about the journey. "We are getting close, are you ready?"

"I'm ready," Samy said confidently.

"Remember Samy, It's not the destination"

"I know Grandpa... it's the journey."

The subdivision we live in has hiking trails, wooded areas, wooden bridges, and streams. There is a field adjacent to the woods that must have been deemed "unbuildable" for some reason. This field has huge boulders that appear to be piercing the surface of the dirt from below. Along the path that borders it, you can see many strata of rock. This is where the heavy equipment must have sheared the rock to create the path and the street adjacent to it when the property was being developed.

Samy and I were on a mission he knew very little about. As we approached the field, he saw the four to six foot high wall of rock in front of us. It was the kind of thing you could walk past every day and not give much thought to, unless of course you were building a mountain and you wanted to identify rock that was native to a particular area.

"Well, what do you think?" I asked.

"Grandpa, this is so cool! Look, you can see different layers of rock just like in the pictures I saw."

"What about the colors in these rocks, are they what you had in mind for our mountain?"

"The colors are perfect they are all different shades of brown and light brown."

There were thin slivers of rock that had fallen to the base of the rock wall we were standing in front of. We picked up quite a few to bring back to our layout where we could properly examine them and possibly use a few at the base of our mountain. We climbed to the top of the wall and sat on a boulder. This gave us a clear view of the entire field and the woods surrounding it.

§

"Can you imagine what this area was like 150 years ago?" Samy said as we sat together surveying the area.

"There were no houses, roads, or cars, just an occasional farm house. Woods and only the crudest of trails worn by horses and horse-drawn carriages separated people. The neighbors you did have might be miles away, but knew one another better than we know our neighbors."

"How did people get to know their neighbors so well? They were so far from one another," Samy asked somewhat confused at the paradox implied in his grandfather's description of our area in the mid 1800's.

"To accurately answer that I would have to go into much greater detail about the fabric of American society at the time we are talking about. It was a much more basic time and if you needed help with something you relied on your neighbor who was only too happy to do so."

I wanted to take advantage of this moment sitting on the rock that day. I also wanted it to be an experience that would help my grandson grow in every way. How often do moments like these present themselves?

"Do you remember a time when Mom ran out of something when she was making dinner?"

"Sure Grandpa that happens sometimes."

"What does she do? I asked.

"She would get in the car and drive to the supermarket," thinking there was more to the question than there was.

"What if there were no roads, cars, or supermarkets?" I said hoping to provoke Samy into thinking.

"I guess people had to do things themselves, like grow their own food, raise animals, chop firewood and even build their own houses," Samy said as he responded much faster than I expected.

"You are absolutely right, and speaking of building houses or barns it was not uncommon for people to come from miles away to help. They did not pick up a phone and call a contractor, electrician, or plumber."

"Was the railroad here yet?"

"The railroad came in 1874 so if we go back 150 years it would be 1860."

"So it was almost here?" Samy asked.

"Almost, it was a very different time and a different way of life from ours."

Samy and I packed up our latest samples and decided to head back to our base. We were both satisfied that we had accomplished our "mission" and had a great time doing so. When we were able to see the house, we saw Grandma standing on the front porch. This reminded both of us of the time we went on another "expedition" and we told Grandma we would be back in about an hour. Three hours later we were greeted by a very worried Grandma who was torn between being happy to see us and sending us both to our rooms!

§

"Where were you two for so long?" Grandma asked.

Sam and I looked at one another and grinned because we knew she would be worried because we agreed that is what grandmothers do.

"We can't tell you everything, but we were on a mission that has something to do with archaeological research for our project."

"Yes and the history of this whole area," Samy responded enthusiastically.

"Do you want to eat lunch now that your 'mission' is over?" Grandma asked.

We both agreed to have lunch and went inside with Grandma. We brought our samples upstairs first of course, to analyze them later. It had been an exciting and productive day and during lunch, we decided to give Grandma a higher security clearance so we could tell her about our expedition. Samy went into detail about the mountain we were about to build, the color of the rock, and the field we found next to the rock wall. He told her about the history of the town and how different it was 150 years ago. His detailed explanations and accounts of what life was like impressed Grandma and she marveled at how factually correct his accounts of what he had read and what we had seen were.

§

The highlight of my day was sitting on that rock with my grandson having a conversation about what life was like one hundred and fifty years ago. These are the "snapshots in time" I share with Samy, that I am confident will never be forgotten. My grandson's appreciation for history, his values, and strength of character are as strong as the rock we sat on that day.

*"Our hearts grow tender with childhood memories
and love of kindred, and we are better throughout
the year for having, in spirit, become a child again at
Christmas time"*

LAURA INGALLS WILDER

CHAPTER 9

Childhood Memories

The delightful smell of the Christmas tree greeted me as I awoke this morning. The house was permeated by the delicious fragrance of a pine forest on a crisp wintery day. It was Christmas Eve, and like so many before it, the excitement, preparation, and anticipation have always remained very special. The house with all of its decorations looked and smelled like something out of a Norman Rockwell painting. Indeed, this was a very special time of year whether you are 6 or 60!

As had been the custom for a number of years, we were going to church and then to our daughter's house for Christmas Eve dinner. Grandma was putting some "finishing touches" on presents she had wrapped and I went upstairs to make sure my camera was ready for tonight's festivities. As I walked by the train room, I saw "Old Bob' sitting on the track looking somewhat lonely. I thought "It may have taken only 60 years but by tomorrow you may have some company."

Could it be possible that memories of events that took place sixty years ago could remain as vivid as those that took place only sixty days ago? My thoughts and memories of Christmas Eve sixty years ago were as clear in my mind as Christmas Eve last year. The sights, sounds, and smells of my boyhood home flooded my mind.

I remembered how patient my father was when our family would go out to purchase the family Christmas tree each year. The weather was always cold and many times, we would do so after a snowfall or even while it was still snowing. I remember quite clearly visiting the tree lots with my family. Each of these lots always seemed to have a fire burning in what appeared to be a fifty-gallon drum. There were strings of lights over the trees to illuminate them for prospective buyers, and assist them in making their choice of a Christmas tree. Tightly strung rope held the trees in place and they were arranged according to size. Dad would pick out a tree from the rows of trees, shake it, and wait for everyone's approval. My older sister who was the most critical, would usually ask him to pick out another and I would only give my approval to the most crooked or sparse trees. This was clearly something my older sister did not appreciate.

Samy loved hearing these stories and always asked to hear more. The older the story the better he seemed to like it. There was an exception to this and the exception was any story that had to do with his mother when she was growing up.

I remembered decorating the family Christmas tree with my family in the small living room of our home. I especially remember how my sister who was five years older than me, always insisted that the tinsel be perfectly placed on each branch of the tree. My older sister's "tinsel technique" provided me with all the motivation necessary to develop a technique of my own. I would "pitch" the tinsel as if I were on the mound for the New York Yankees, which had the predictable result of driving my sister wild. This I did when I "thought" my parents were not looking.

I also remember a dream I had when I was Samy's age about how I saw Santa. The dream was so real that when I woke up Christmas morning I remember telling my mother, father, sister, or anyone who would listen, every single detail!

These and many other childhood memories Samy always enjoyed hearing about. Samy considered me the ultimate resource when it came to stories of this nature. When placed in the proper context these stories about family can provide valuable lessons to our children and grandchildren.

§

Time passed very quickly that day and before we knew it, we were ringing the doorbell at my daughter's house. I heard the unmistakable footsteps of my favorite soccer player gliding across the floor. The door opened and Samy wished us a "Merry Christmas" and gave us each a hug. It wasn't long before everyone had arrived. Samy's cousins and close friends were now there and the house was filled with the sound of children laughing and playing on Christmas Eve.

Several times over the course of the evening, Samy came over to me and said, "Grandpa, do you think Santa is going to bring me The Milwaukee?"

"I'm sure he will do his best, but we will know for sure tomorrow morning."

Early that evening, Samy had taken me aside and expressed concern that he was not able to give people he loved such as his mother and father, a gift for Christmas they truly deserved. These sentiments were expressed by my grandson when he said, "Grandpa, Mommy and Daddy do so much they should get a present for Christmas just like me." His sincere expression told me that my six-year-old grandson had indeed learned the true meaning of Christmas at a very young age, and one unfortunately some never learn.

"You may not realize it now, Samy, but what you have just said will be the greatest gift you could possibly give."

"But Grandpa I still don't have a present for them to open."

"Sometimes the best presents we give are not the ones we can wrap, they are the things we actually do, Samy."

I went on to summarize a story about a young boy who lived over one hundred years ago. He was very poor and lived on a farm with his parents. Every morning this young boy, who was twice your age, would have to get up very early in the morning to help his father milk the cows and do other chores with his father. His father disliked waking his son so early in the morning but needed his help. "You see Samy his father loved him very much."

"Did this boy get his father a present on Christmas?" Samy asked.

"This young boy felt very much like you do."

"In what way did this little boy feel like me, Grandpa?"

On Christmas Eve the young boy overheard his father telling his mother how much he did not want to wake his son on Christmas morning to do chores, but he really needed him to help. This gave the young boy an idea. He knew how hard his father worked and he wanted to do something for him especially on Christmas. He decided to get up at three in the morning instead of five when his father called him. He would do all the milking of the cows and any other chores before his father woke him up. He was awake at one, two, and finally at three in the morning he quietly went into the barn and milked every cow, and completed all the chores they would normally do together. Quietly, he got back into bed and when his father called him, he told his father he would meet him in the barn shortly.

When his father saw what his son had done for him it brought tears to his eyes. The young boy met his father in the barn that morning and his father told him as he hugged him tightly that this was the best Christmas present he had ever received in his entire life. Actually, he would continue to tell everyone for years to come what his son had done for him.

"This young boy could not give his father a present to open, so he did something for him," Samy said with a tone that indicated he still wished he could do more.

"I saw the beautiful card you made for Mom and Dad and the cookies you helped Mom bake for Santa. Let's not forget the great report cards you bring home from school. These are the things you do every day Mom and Dad really love."

I will never get used to the responses Samy gives me, nor do I want to. Samy looked at me, gave me a hug, and said, "I love you Grandpa."

"I love you too, but will you help me milk the cows?" I asked.

"A whole barn full of cows, Grandpa!"

I knew then that Samy understood the meaning of the story I had just told him. This was one of the "snapshots in time" that will remain in our hearts forever.

§

After we had eaten dinner, it was time to play the "White Elephant" game that everyone was looking forward to playing. Samy and his dad were cutting up numbers to be given to everyone for the "White Elephant" presents. Each person was given a slip of paper with a number on it. This number determined the order in which each participant chose their present. The idea was to wrap something you would not ordinarily buy as a present or something you thought was silly like an ugly necktie. The only limit was your imagination.

Everyone was having a great time, however it wasn't long before Santa would be visiting each of us. It was time to leave and prepare for his arrival. We all knew what was on our children's minds tonight. Samy said goodbye to everyone, and wished his cousins, aunts, and uncles a "Merry Christmas" as they left to go home to bed on this very special night. As we were leaving, we wished everyone a Merry Christmas and Samy gave us a big hug.

"Did you get your milk, and cookies ready for Santa?" Grandma asked.

"Yes, I helped Mom bake them today and we are going to leave them right on the table near the tree," Samy said with a great deal of excitement in his voice.

"Great, now promise us you will call us in the morning and we will see you tomorrow."

"I promise to call you as soon as I get up," Samy said very excited that Santa would be visiting him soon!

§

The excitement and bright-eyed enthusiasm we saw in Samy's eyes that night reminded us of our own children on Christmas Eve. It brought back memories of when Grandma and Grandpa were Samy's age as well! This was one of those special moments in our lives when the "magic" of Christmas as seen through the eyes of a six year old touches us all! These are the "snapshots in time" we will cherish forever!

"Happy, happy Christmas, that can recall to the older man the pleasures of his youth; that can transport the traveler back to his own fireside and his quiet home"

CHARLES DICKENS

CHAPTER 10

A Magical Time of Year

Who doesn't remember the thrill of getting up on Christmas morning and racing to the Christmas tree to see what Santa brought us? Christmas morning for those who celebrate Christmas, was a magical time. There are those who say that the joy of waking up on Christmas morning diminishes with age, and the magic somehow loses its sparkle. I believe that we pass on this "magic" by creating this joy for our children and grandchildren.

Hope, joy, and excitement fill the air on this very special morning. Regardless of our age, we still enjoy all of the things we remember from our childhood about Christmas morning. We never tire of opening presents with our family members and most of all sharing memories of other Christmas mornings past.

The smell of a fire burning in the fireplace, special foods Mom cooked, the Christmas tree, Christmas music, and going to church with family are all part of what made Christmas morning so special to so many people around the world. Christmas morning was also a time to get together with relatives and friends, showing love for one another with good conversation and laughter.

I remember with stunning clarity, the Christmas mornings when I would position myself strategically with my camera so I could get a photograph of my children rubbing their sleepy eyes and capturing the moment when they got their first glimpse of what Santa had left them for Christmas. These are the moments we never forget and as we grow older we create them for our children and grandchildren. Many of us have entire photo albums devoted to Christmas and others are fortunate to have not only still photos but videos also!

§

I also remember that my Jewish friends when Hanukkah was close to or overlapped with Christmas, loved the season perhaps as much as I did. Something in the back of my mind secretly wished for all to celebrate their respective holidays together. It seemed to make so much sense, especially when you are six years old.

There is no doubt that we have commercialized Christmas to the point where some times the true meaning is forgotten. Under the guidance of parents and grandparents this does not have to be. Christmas is about "giving" not just about "receiving" presents. In this respect, I am proud that my grandson knows the true meaning of Christmas and he has experienced the true joy of "giving" every day of the year.

§

I had awakened several times during the night for no apparent reason. Perhaps my subconscious was urging me to look under the Christmas tree to see what Santa had left me. Was it the sound of reindeer on the roof? I did not know for sure until the phone rang very early Christmas morning. I quickly reached for the phone and said "Merry Christmas." The voice at the other end of the line seemed to have trouble forming his words and said excitedly, "Grandpa, guess what Santa left me last night?"

"Let's see... I know you are a good boy so it couldn't have been coal, give me a minute and..." Samy was not about to wait a second longer and he answered immediately. He was thrilled with his present from Santa.

"The Milwaukee Engine and he brought some cars to go with it and they even match the engine!"

"Wow, Samy that is absolutely fantastic!" I said excitedly.

"It's orange and black and has the rails around it just like the one we saw on the computer. I think the number is the exact same one, it is number 8858!"

"I think you are right Samy. The number sounds right to me."

"He even set it up on the track for me with the transformer and all."

"It looks like 'Old Bob' will have some company after all." I said, happy that my grandson was so thrilled with the present Santa had left for him. Samy was not the only one thrilled that Santa had brought the Milwaukee Engine.

"It goes really fast, and it looks great." Samy said enthusiastically.

"I can't wait. I'll be over as soon as you can say Milwaukee!"

The excitement in his voice was contagious and brought out the little boy who on this day sixty years ago was the recipient of "Old Bob."

§

One of the greatest "perks" of living in the subdivision we do is that Grandma and I are so close to our grandson.

Samy had recently moved into the same subdivision that Grandma and I live in. He is now only a short walk away from us. Most of our friends have grandchildren that live hours or days away from them. We are extremely fortunate to be able to be a part of every milestone in our grandson's life. We are able to share school functions, soccer games, birthdays, and holidays with Samy. Actually, we feel badly for those who cannot. I could not imagine living far away from my grandson.

I hurriedly jumped into the shower and was dressed in minutes. The garage door opened and it was only then that I realized that the sun was just starting to come up. I started the car and was on my way. As I backed out of the driveway, my thoughts turned to the child born in a manger over two thousand years ago, and how appropriate it was that Christmas should be celebrated through the eyes of a child, and how the gift was not a train, but a blessing called Samy.

§

"You won't believe how fast this train goes. It will have no trouble pulling freight up our hill and through the mountains," Samy said enthusiastically as he greeted me at the door.

The Milwaukee looked better in person than it did in the pictures we had seen. It was a highly detailed replica of the real Milwaukee diesel. It was exact in every detail as the one that had graced the tracks for so many years. I too was excited to see that Santa had left Samy such a beautiful addition to his train layout.

"Let me see what the Milwaukee can do, Samy."

"Watch this, Grandpa," Samy said confidently.

Samy gradually raised the lever on the transformer and the engine began to move forward slowly. His excitement increased as he raised the lever and the engine's speed increased. The Milwaukee was taking the turns smoothly and at a much faster speed than I thought was possible.

"This is the fastest engine I have ever seen," Samy said as the Milwaukee cruised effortlessly around the track.

"It is surely not like "Old Bob" when he was new. I remember having to keep the speed way down, or he would fall off the tracks."

"Not the Milwaukee, Grandpa, and it's pulling five cars!"

We sat there for almost an hour and watched the Milwaukee engine go around the track. The two of us observed it from every possible angle and marveled at its ability handle the turns just the way its real-life counterpart would. Even with a full load of matchbox cars in the car carrier, the Milwaukee performed flawlessly.

"I like the matching Milwaukee caboose, Samy."

"It is the same color as the engine and has the same rails around it."

"You made a good choice and I am sure "Old Bob" will be happy to have some company."

This was one of those moments in time that our children and grandchildren will always remember. Our shared enthusiasm for working together was something that brought us closer and I was sure we would never forget. Samy and I knew it was not the train or the layout that was important. It wouldn't be the mountain we were about to build or the village either. Samy may have been slightly under seven years old at the time, but I knew he understood clearly when I said to him, "It's not the destination, it's the journey."

"I have to go now but I will return as quickly as I can with Grandma who has some very special Christmas presents for you."

§

Grandma and I returned later with presents, wrapped with love by Grandma. Samy opened the door for us and helped us in with the gifts. Samy helped put them all under the Christmas tree.

"A couple of those are very special, and I think you will be very excited when you open them."

"Do you mean the socks and the underwear?" Samy responded with his dimples showing.

"I'm not sure they are that special but we shall see."

I had told Samy many times when I was growing up and even when I was an adult, my mother would always give me something like socks and underwear. It had become almost a tradition as well as an amusing family story. One can only imagine the priority these presents had in comparison to the Milwaukee. The humor was certainly not lost on him.

We said our prayers of gratitude for all that we had and prayed for those who did not. The food my daughter prepared was as delicious as always. It was good to see everyone so happy and as a grandfather it was especially gratifying. My thoughts at times like these often turn to those who are not so fortunate and do not possess all that we have. Wealth, is too often is measured by the amount of money an individual accumulates. I did not have to check my bank account to know. All I had to do was look around the table to know just how blessed and truly well-off I was!

We all gathered near the tree to open our presents. This was a special time for me because I was surrounded by those I loved.

"This one's for you, Samy," Grandma said as she gave the present to Samy.

"This could be one of those "special" presents we talked about," I said.

"Oh Grandpa...."

He tore open the wrapping paper and out came a model airplane kit. This scene was repeated many times for Samy and each time he thanked Mom, Dad, Grandma, Grandpa, or Aunt Michelle for his gift.

Everyone was finished exchanging gifts when I said to Samy, "It's time for your special present from Grandma!"

"I think I know what it is," he said with a sheepish grin.

He tore off the wrapping paper and there they were! Socks and underwear were presents that topped all seven-year-olds' lists to Santa! With as much excitement as he could, Samy thanked Grandma for his gift.

"It is not the mountain we conquer but ourselves"
EDMUND HILLARY

CHAPTER 11

Climb Every Mountain

S amy and I were both excited about building the mountain for our train layout. We had done a considerable amount of research and knew that the mountain would be the most prominent feature on our layout. It was important that we build something that would be impressive and functional since we planned to have our train pass through it on two levels. This necessitated the incorporation of two tunnels at precisely the correct locations to accommodate the trains that would soon be passing through them. Above all, we did not want our mountain to look like those we saw for sale on the internet. The goal was to create something that was realistic and true to scale.

This was the beginning of a truly exciting and creative phase of our journey together. Neither of us realized at this point how imaginative and fun this was going to be. The approach we had taken thus far included much planning and research. We studied the history of the time period, discussed the scale of our models, and we were committed to making everything on our layout as detailed and accurate as possible. Now we were able to combine our planning and research with creativity and imagination to make our layout come to life!

This was the next phase of our master plan and it was now time to build the highly anticipated and often discussed mountain. The mountain had been the subject of much revision especially details such as the height, length, width and tunnel placement. We planned to have two tunnels through our mountain. Samy and I had researched the composition, scale, and area of the country we wanted our mountain to resemble. The rocks we had gathered were still on our layout and remained a source of inspiration for us. Memories of our "expedition" to gather our samples were still fresh in our minds.

§

We selected the right rear corner of our layout as the site for the mountain in order to have an unobstructed view of our entire train layout with the mountain serving as a magnificent backdrop for the woodlands and village below. The only thing that remained was to build it. I was looking forward to building the mountain with my grandson as much as he was looking forward to building it.

"Samy, let's go into the garage and see if I have a thin sheet of plywood."

"We are going to build the mountain out of plywood?" he asked, somewhat confused at the choice of building materials.

"I think it may be a good idea if we built the mountain on the plywood and then we can bring it up to our layout when we are done. Some of the material we will be using like the plaster cloth can become very messy."

We went into the garage together and found a great piece of plywood for our mountain. It was approximately 34 inches square. We cut it diagonally and had the perfect base for our mountain. Samy was looking at the 34 inch square that was now 2 pieces when he said "Grandpa now we have two triangles instead of one square."

"Do you know what the line I drew inside the square is called?"

"I think it's called a diagonal," Samy answered after pausing to think for a moment.

"That is excellent Samy, you should be proud of yourself."

"Thanks Grandpa we learned about some figures and shapes in school."

"Here is what I want you to do. First, measure each of the sides of the triangle and write down the measurements. Then measure the length of the diagonal we cut and write that down," I said while handing the tape measure to Samy.

Samy knew I was going somewhere with this and it probably was going to be fun so he followed my instructions to the letter and said, "What do I do next Grandpa?"

"Just hand me the paper and we will get back to it later, right now we have a mountain to build."

"Should we bring the base upstairs and put the track on it so we know where the tunnel should go?"

"You never cease to amaze me, Samy that is an excellent idea!"

We brought our base upstairs and slid it under the track on the layout so Samy could mark off the curve of the track with a pencil. Afterwards he drew straight lines 3 inches on either side of the track where we would screw in the sides of our tunnel.

"Great lines, Samy are you ready to go back to the shop?"

"Are we going to put the side pieces on now?" Samy asked, excited to complete the tunnel section.

"Let's measure the pieces we need first and we'll cut them in the garage and put them together."

When the sides of the tunnel and the top were complete we screwed them into place and stepped back to admire our work. Even the angles came out great and we congratulated each other for a job well done. We were looking forward to the next phase of our mountain project because we both agreed that this is when our mountain would look like the real thing. Samy commented that our creation thus far looked like anything but a mountain!

"Samy, I almost forgot" I said, eyeing the piece of 1 inch x 2 inch x 29 inch lumber I had cut.

"What is that for? Is that the height of the mountain?" Samy asked and answered his own question.

"I'm going to screw this on the backside of our tunnel side and it will become the height of the mountain. You were right, it will determine the height of the mountain."

As Samy watched the board sliding into place, I was not sure he understood the purpose of this board until he said, "So the top of that board is the peak and we staple the screening to the top and bring it down all over!"

I looked at Samy, paused for a moment, and said "I should have known better. Your assessment of the purpose of this board is exactly correct and now I might even tell you why I had you write those numbers down."

We both laughed and Samy smiled proudly. The mountain we had talked so much about building was finally starting to take shape and we could not have been happier!

§

We brought our mountain inside, assembled all our materials on the kitchen floor, filled the tray that Grandma gave us with water and were ready to build our mountain. Admittedly, we joked that our mountain looked like anything but a mountain now, but in an hour or so, we would have a first class large mountain with all of the topographical features we had discussed!

The next step was to staple the screening to form the inner skin of the mountain. We cut a very large piece of screening and draped it over the 29 inch piece of lumber such that in back it would reach the plywood base. Staples were placed on top and along the base in back leaving ample ripples in the screen. Our frame for the oversized tunnel we had built supported the front of the screen. There was a more gradual descent on this side of the mountain, for it contained all the ridges, plateaus, and landforms you would expect to find on a mountain. Samy held the screening in place and I began to staple the edges to the platform. Unbelievably, our creation was starting to look like a mountain, and a good one at that!

"Samy check this out, I am going to start 'molding' our peak." As I was speaking, I was squeezing the screening in to the shape we wanted for the peak of the mountain.

"That is so cool, Grandpa!" Samy exclaimed with a great deal of enthusiasm.

"You take over, and remember to allow for the stream we want that will eventually lead to our waterfall on the right side."

Samy took over and began "sculpting" the mountain as if he had been doing it for years. We then talked about how we wanted the mountain to look and where to put the small plateaus, ridges, and small mountain streams. Samy caught on quickly and began to mold the screen and made a gradual descent down one side and then the other. When we were satisfied we had included all of the features we wanted, including a waterfall, we put a few more strategically placed staples in. Samy made some minor adjustments in our sculpture and we were ready to begin to apply the plaster cloth that would become the surface of our mountain!

We brought the plaster cloth rolls we had purchased into the kitchen and began to pass the plaster cloth strips we had cut through the water. Each strip was carefully placed on the skeleton of our mountain. We completed the back and about 8 inches down the mountain when we stopped to admire our work.

"Grandpa, this looks even better than a real mountain. The ridges and depressions look so real!"

"I have to agree, it is coming out great! Did you want to stop for today?" I asked knowing what Samy's answer would be.

"I want to finish it today!" Samy answered as he applied another piece of plaster cloth to our mountain.

"You are doing a great job on this, Samy, and I think we will be finished today, although I think you missed a spot."

"Where did I miss Grandpa?"

"Right here," as I dabbed the end of his nose with a little plaster.

Samy returned the favor and we worked the rest of the afternoon with those plaster noses. Each piece brought us closer to completing our mountain.

"Samy, it looks like we're finished and I will let you have the honor of putting on the last piece."

Samy laid the last piece on the mountain and we looked at one another and just smiled. Samy wanted to put on a couple of finishing touches by "smoothing out" a few areas where the plaster was thicker. He put a few drops of water on those areas and smoothed them out with his fingers.

"You have done a great job and I think you are becoming a world-class sculptor."

"Thanks Grandpa, you are to."

"Is that a good shirt you have on? If it is I think both of us may be in trouble."

He laughed and said, "Mommy told me I could get plaster on this or paint and it would be O.K."

"Between the two of us we probably have as much plaster on us as half the mountain!" I said laughing and knowing that it was all part of the fun!

"How soon will it be dry?" Samy asked as he continued to smooth out the rough spots and seams with additional water. He added strips of plaster cloth to form the streams we needed for our waterfalls and touched up the sides of the tunnel.

"I would estimate between 24 to 36 hours to dry and 3 days before we can paint. We should experiment with mixing paint in order to get the exact color we want."

"That's perfect Grandpa, because there is no school on Monday and we will be able to paint our mountain" Samy replied with his characteristic enthusiasm that had served us so well on our "journey" thus far.

"That sounds good to me. We should check to make sure we have the right colors of paint to mix."

"This is going to be the best train layout ever, this mountain looks so cool, and it was so much fun to do!"

"I will say one thing Samy, we haven't seen anything this big or detailed anywhere we looked online."

§

No words were necessary to describe our time together. The looks on our faces said it all. We had a phenomenal time together that afternoon and this was one of those "snapshots in time" we will always remember. Samy slid our creation into the corner of the breakfast area of the kitchen and cleaned the excess plaster we had spilled on the kitchen floor with a sponge and I dried it off with some paper towels.

Our "clean-up" was complete. Grandma came into the kitchen to admire our creation and said, "Not only is your mountain beautiful but it is so lifelike. Did you follow plans for building it?"

Samy quickly replied to Grandma's comment about plans. "Oh no Grandma our entire mountain is original and we created it ourselves. We looked on the internet and our mountain is one hundred times better than the mountains we saw."

"Now that I look carefully at your mountain, it is probably is a thousand times better. Everything on it is so realistic including the rock formations and the streams you built in to it. I love the tunnels you built for the train to pass through. I am really impressed with the work you have done!" Grandma was clearly impressed as she stepped back to admire our tunnel again.

"Thanks Grandma, we had so much fun doing it that Grandpa said we should go into the 'mountain-building business' and sell them on eBay."

"Thank you for doing such a great job cleaning up. The tile looks great," Grandma said as she gave Samy a kiss.

§

Samy had demonstrated his ability to see things in his "mind's eye" and create them from there, losing nothing in the translation. Children show these creative and imaginative abilities when they are given opportunities to use them. I knew that if it were not a mountain, we would have built something else. It did seem appropriate that we should build a mountain together. Mountains were symbolic with "challenge", and there was nothing Samy and I liked better than a good challenge. We felt as though we were standing on the summit of a mountain we had just climbed!

Topographical features, landforms, mountain streams, vocabulary, scale, imagination, and creativity all come to mind when I think back to that day. The blessing, who I call Samy, is what I am thankful for every day. We have become carpenters, engineers, researchers, train experts, and now "world-class" sculptors. The titles we value the most are "Grandson" and "Grandpa"!

"Life is divided into three terms, that which was, which is, and which will be. Let us learn from the past to profit by the present, and from the present, to live better in the future."

WILLIAM WORDSWORTH

CHAPTER 12

A Page From The History Books

The years between 1860 and 1920 have often been referred to as "The Golden Age of Railroads." This was a time when the railroad was having a profound effect on America's growing economy and way of life. Although they existed in the early to mid-1800s, the railroads were now giving much more thought to connecting with one another and spanning the entire country.

This was an era in American history that through our research about railroads fascinated both of us. We also became acquainted with the history of the very town in which we live. By the early 1800s this rich and attractive land on which our town was built had attracted settlers who began to clear land for farming. Prior to 1874, transportation to this area was by horse or stagecoach only. The first railroad came to our once sleepy little town in 1874. It was in this year that this town we now call home was connected to all other areas of the country.

We discovered that ten of the original buildings built in the center of our town still exist today. The Baptist, Methodist and Presbyterian churches established in 1877 remain on their original sites as well. The most intriguing historical landmark to us was the hardware or "general merchandise" store that is still in operation today! Immediately it moved up to number one on our "places to visit" list.

This wasn't just "any" historical landmark, but one that had just stepped off the pages of the history books. We were viewing an historical landmark that exists not more than two miles away from us in the same town we live in. We examined the pictures of all of these historic landmarks on the computer and read about their history. It was hard to believe that we had driven past them so many times. Neither of us had ever been to this hardware store, but suddenly we couldn't wait to get there. The more we read about its history and looked at the photographs taken in the early 1900s as well as the present, the more our interest grew. What we didn't know was just how impressed we would be!

§

The exterior of the building had not changed since 1900. As we gazed at the building and looked in the windows, our appreciation for what has been preserved here grew exponentially. The very first steps we took greeted us with a "creak" as we walked on the original hardwood floors. It was somewhat difficult to believe that artisans in the year 1900, well over one hundred years ago, installed the very same floor we were now walking on. The shelves were stocked from floor to ceiling with all manner of nails and general hardware that cannot be found in the "big box" stores. There were canning supplies and seeds for anything that will grow in the ground. The display of cast iron cookware was amazing. This sight was common 75 years ago, but extremely rare today. Feed for wild birds, poultry, and rabbits were also on display, along with every conceivable birdhouse or bird feeder imaginable. If you are looking for live bait, this store can accommodate you.

If you are thirsty, one of the first refrigerated soda machines made is still in operation there now. The same scales used at the turn of the century, weigh bulk nails and other items today. The experience of seeing all of this could not have been better even if we did have a "time machine" that allowed us to go back to the year 1900!

Samy and I toured the entire store more than once. We marveled at the product selection. We truly had gone back in time to a much simpler life. This general merchandise store had not changed and remained as it was at the turn of the century.

It was winter and we eventually found ourselves seated in front of the same pot-bellied stove that so many customers had gathered around since 1900. Yes, it was the original pot-bellied stove! "Grandpa this stove is keeping the whole store warm." Samy commented on how evenly distributed the heat from the stove was and how in some ways it heated the store better than modern heating systems.

We sat in front of that pot-bellied stove for at least thirty minutes and all that we were experiencing mesmerized both of us. This was truly something you could not learn from a textbook. This had to be experienced and I could not think of anyone I would rather experience it with.

The sights, sounds, and smells told us we had gone back in time over 110 years. What we had found was nothing short of amazing. Our journey had taken us to a place in time Samy and I did not expect.

"Grandpa, I don't believe how many really cool things are in here and how everything is the same for over a hundred years!"

"Just think for a moment, we could be a couple of farmers in let's say 1902 talking about buying seed to plant in the spring."

"Our horses would be tied outside, right Grandpa?"

"That's right and you could buy feed for them right here. We could purchase saddles and feed for our horses. Did you know that farmers did not always pay when they purchased seed to plant?"

"How did the owner get paid for what they bought?" Samy asked.

"They would sign a receipt and after they harvested and sold their crops they would come in to pay. Money rarely changed hands and of course there were no credit cards."

"What happened if they didn't pay?"

"That rarely happened and when it did it was because the crop was not good that year and the farmer would pay him back when he could."

"Can we come back here again, because there are so many things in here that we couldn't have seen everything?" Samy asked wide-eyed and inquisitively.

"I think we have found the closest thing we will ever find to our time machine, and of course we'll come back. One visit is not enough to appreciate this piece of history we have in the center of our very own town."

As we were leaving two of the people who were working there said goodbye to us and told us to come again to visit. We thanked them and said we sure would.

"They said goodbye when we were leaving the store but it sounded the same way as when you leave someone's house," Samy said as we reached the sidewalk.

"Your very perceptive, Samy, in some ways that is their house and it's been in their family for generations. I was reading about their history and before the last remaining heir died the present owner bought this store. He worked here when he was young and used to cut the grass at the last surviving heir's house. When he graduated from college, he decided to buy the business. He was the closest thing to "family" you could be. He had a long relationship with the descendants of the original owners."

We walked about fifty yards up this historical street together and we both knew that we had just stepped off a page in the history of America. We were about to turn that page and step onto another.

§

The very same roadbed that was home to the tracks built in 1874 was before us as we proceeded up the street. These tracks, just like the hardware store we had come from remain in operation today. We crossed the tracks and walked along the roadbed to the old train depot which had also been preserved and serves as a museum for the history of railroads.

We toured the building and noted that those same original hardwood floors also greeted us with a creak. Next to the train depot was a red caboose from the 1870s that had been restored and stood next to that train depot as if it were standing guard for its old friend.

"Grandpa, the more I look at these buildings the more I would like to put them on our layout."

"In other words, you would like the same style of architecture and the same time period." I was happy that Samy evidently appreciated much more than just old buildings from the past. He was clearly impressed with the architecture of this period in history.

"Do you remember those 'Americana' buildings we saw?"

"Yes I do Samy," I answered just as I was thinking just how perceptive my grandson was.

"I think they look just like the hardware store and the stores next to it." The buildings Samy was referring to did indeed look very similar to the general merchandise store we had just discovered.

"They do Samy and they are the exact period in history we have been talking about."

"They had an early drug store, a post office, a restaurant and they looked really cool." Samy's interest in the "Americana" buildings increased as we talked.

"Those are the ones that we would have to build because they are not assembled," I stated remembering how detailed and how much work these buildings involved. They involve not only building but also painting, grouting, aging, illuminating, and even decorating the interiors. The more work that was involved in doing something the more Samy liked it. He was never looking for the easiest way but rather as he described it, "The most fun."

A train whistle we heard in the distance interrupted our conversation. We were standing near the old train depot and sure enough, a train was coming. There was a bend in the tracks about a quarter of a mile from where we were standing but we could hear the engine and the unmistakable sound of the wheels on the tracks. First, the engine with its bright light came into view and then one car at a time. The train came around the bend and that great diesel horn sounded just as the crossing gates went down, the lights flashed and the bells warned of the approaching train. The cars on the road stopped to wait for the oncoming train. The timing of this train's arrival could not have been better. We watched until we could not see the caboose in the distance any longer. I could not help but think that my fascination with trains had not diminished since I was Samy's age. What was it about "all things railroad" that fascinated so many people?

The train passed very close to us that day and the look on Samy's face clearly showed his love for trains. "That was so cool Grandpa. That engine was pulling forty cars." He commented that the early trains would have been steam engines instead of the diesel that had just gone by.

"You are right Samy the early engines would have been steam. Depending on the availability and type of fuel they used, steam was a very efficient way to power the engines."

"These can't be the same tracks that were built over one hundred years ago."

"Right again. The rails and the roadbed they are on needed strengthening to accommodate heavier loads as time went on, so they were replaced by newer and stronger rails. The track does follow the original route with a few variations."

"Thanks Grandpa," Samy said seriously.

"Thanks for what?" I had a feeling that what everyone had come to expect and admire about my grandson was the clue to what his answer would be.

"The trip to the hardware store, the station house and the train...and I still can't believe how cool that store is!" Samy exclaimed still excited about what we had seen!

"One hundred years ago on this very spot another grandfather and grandson may have been standing here watching a train pull into the station," I said to my grandson.

Samy wrinkled his forehead paused for a moment and replied "Somehow Grandpa I do not think it would be the same."

"In what ways do you think it would be different, Samy?"

Without hesitation Samy answered "We were both amazed at how everything in the store had stayed the same and we could not get over how we could sit at the same old stove they sat in front of over a hundred years ago. If we went into the store or watched the train pull in over a hundred years ago..." Samy stopped and seemed to be rethinking what he was saying.

"The amazement they felt in 1900 would have come from the train and their new ability to buy things at this general merchandise store they could not have bought before. The railroad was beginning to change their lives in ways they never imagined. Their excitement at what they saw and experienced may have originated from a different source, but they were amazed just as we are." I realized that putting yourself in someone's place was difficult. Walking in someone's shoes that lived over one hundred years ago was especially challenging!

"If they looked back in time they saw just farms and no railroad. Maybe they thought about those times the same way we think about them?"

I wanted to encourage Samy to continue with his exceptionally mature reasoning for someone his age, so

I paused for a moment before I said, "They probably did but they welcomed the railroad because it made their lives better and brought them much-needed necessities like the latest farm tools."

"They were able to send whatever they grew on their farms to places they were not able to send them before."

"Very good Samy you remembered! That was probably the biggest advantage the railroad gave them."

"Thanks Grandpa, I remember reading that in a book that I took out at the library about trains."

§

Samy and I continued our discussion about the railroad, life at the turn of the century, and of course the general merchandise store. About two hours had passed when we were interrupted by the sound of a train whistle once again. The gates went down, the lights began to flash, and the bells went off. We looked toward the bend in the distance, and sure enough, another train was coming around the bend. This time the train made a brief stop next to the station where we were standing and we were treated to an extreme close-up of an enormous diesel engine. The stop however brief was thrilling nonetheless!

"Wow! That was fantastic" Samy said as the train disappeared into the distance and we could see it no longer.

"It sure was, they must have known we were waiting here."

"One hundred years from now another grandfather and grandson might come here to watch the train," Samy commented as he looked up at me.

"Maybe, and I hope they have the same experience we have had together."

I knew that regardless of the century, there was certainly no one I would rather travel through time with than Samy! There are some things in this world that are "timeless" and Samy possessed every one of them. Perhaps one day he will stand with his grandson and share the same privilege I have known.

"In the long run, men hit only what they aim at.
Therefore, they had better aim at something high."
Henry David Thoreau

CHAPTER 13

We "Can" Build It

The mountain we had created had been one of our most enjoyable experiences. Its peak, ridges and plateaus were extremely detailed and realistic. The coloration of its rock formations had been a success and we were both happy with the result of our work. There was no doubt that we had created something that we could not purchase anywhere. The memories of our mountain were forever etched in our hearts and minds.

Since that first day we had added a larger plateau toward the left side of the mountain to accommodate a log cabin and another toward the right side to allow for our waterfall that would cascade into a lake below. The addition of our "mountain range" made it easy to create the tunnel for the lower section of track. These mountain "structures" were done with our mountain in place on our layout. Samy had become quite good at plaster work and sculpting the ridges. It never ceases to amaze me the abilities that children have. The only things that are lacking sometimes are the opportunities to use them.

"Grandpa, how are we going to get two levels?"

"Here's the plan. Listen and tell me what you think. We need a roadbed approximately five inches high, so the plan is to use boards around the whole layout and screw them in from the bottom and then attach the roadbed board to the sides."

"Won't that look like too much wood and not real?" Samy inquired.

"It would if we just left it like that but this gives us an opportunity to place rocks along the roadbed and shrubs and all sorts of things you would find on a mountain pass."

"We could use the rocks from the rock molds we made," Samy said enthusiastically.

"I think you've got it, Samy."

"We could use the rocks we collected on our expeditions and some of the rocks from the backyard." Samy replied, proud that he had remembered the rocks he and I had collected on one of our expeditions together.

"This can't be any harder than the mountain we just built and the two tunnels that were formed when we added to our mountain." We were now confident in our ability to create even the most complex structures.

"When can we start putting up the sides?" Samy replied with his usual enthusiasm and desire to get things done.

"Follow me, we need some real muscle for this." He laughed and followed me out of the room.

We went downstairs and Samy explained in detail to Grandma what we were planning. I was not sure she knew what he was talking about, but Grandma did get us to eat lunch. This gave us an opportunity to talk more about the scenery that was sure to make our railroad good enough to be on the cover of any model railroad magazine.

"Let's go to the garage. I took the liberty of cutting the boards we will need this morning before you came."

"Great, now we can put them up!" Samy said with his usual enthusiasm.

We carried the pieces of pre-cut lumber upstairs and then went back for the drills. Samy had no trouble carrying any of our supplies. His enthusiasm is contagious and he has always been grateful for the opportunities he is presented.

"Cross your fingers and hope this works. It has to be strong enough to hold the board which will become our roadbed as well as the weight of the train." I may have been kidding but realized that "many a truth were said in jest".

"Don't worry Grandpa, I have confidence in you." Samy said while laughing!

"Oh really, then what are you laughing about?" I replied.

"I just thought about..." Samy quickly replied.

"Sure you did" I said as we both were laughing.

§

When we reached our layout, I positioned the boards in place and showed Samy how I intended to use long screws from underneath to hold them in place.

"First we position the board on the edge of the layout and make sure it is even and then I will drill the pilot holes from underneath. Before we do anything it might be a good idea to position the boards perfectly and draw a pencil line on the table top so both sides of the board can be seen."

"Won't the boards fall when you start to drill?" Samy asked with a somewhat quizzical look on his face.

"That's where you come in, Samy. You hold them perfectly straight and I will drill from below."

"Should I push down on them so they won't slip at all?" Samy asked.

"That is a great idea, all you have to do is apply enough pressure to hold them in place, and the drill will do the rest."

We lined up the "walls" at the edges of our layout and Samy held them in place as I drilled the pilot holes from below. After each hole was drilled a 3 inch screw was put in from below. We chose to put in screws every two feet and add more if necessary. When we were finished with the first board we checked it for strength to make sure it would hold our roadbed securely!

"Grandpa, I can't believe how strong this board is!" Samy said as he tugged on the board.

"This came out much stronger than I thought it would. I really was planning on putting in more screws."

We repeated this process until we had completely finished all sides of our layout. We pushed on each board to make sure each was strong enough to hold the roadway we were about to erect on all sides. One hour later our layout had an upper level!

"Grandpa, this looks really great and the upper level lines up perfectly with the entrance to our mountain tunnel. The train will really look like it is climbing the mountain on the right side because of the way we tilted the roadbed."

§

Samy was right on with his analysis of our mountain pass. The roadbed that would hold our track was inclined just enough to add the beauty and realism we wanted to achieve. I was extremely happy with the strength of the roadbed. "This is strong enough to hold five times the weight of our heaviest engine," I said to Samy.

"This is super strong," Samy replied as he pressed his hand against the roadbed that would be home to our track.

"I couldn't have done it without you!"

"Can we put the track on now?" Samy asked.

"We sure can and we will test it out to make sure it passes the strength test."

We put the track on our new upper level and put our Milwaukee engine on the track. I hooked up the wire to the track and Samy hooked up the transformer side. We were now ready to test our elevated track.

"You have the honor of giving the Milwaukee power to test our elevated track," I said as I turned on the main power switch.

Samy raised the lever on the transformer slowly and the Milwaukee began its gradual ascent on our roadway until it disappeared into the mountain tunnel and reappeared on the other side of the mountain. Watching it go around the elevated track was a beautiful sight indeed.

"Let's hook up the cars and test it with at least 6 cars." Samy said excitedly.

Samy brought the engine around to what was to be our control panel and began hooking up one car after another until he reached for the Milwaukee caboose. With the caboose hooked up securely, he raised the lever and the Milwaukee engine moved forward and effortlessly climbed the elevated track and disappeared into the mountain with its six cars!

"It looks as though we were successful, Samy," I said satisfied that our upper level of track was structurally sound.

"I really like the way we elevated the track more on the back of the layout and how we made the tracks gradually climb up toward the mountain," Samy declared with a look of satisfaction.

"We both want to make sure that the track doesn't need any structural adjustments."

"I don't think it will, Grandpa, it is very strong," Samy said as he checked it once again to make sure.

"Is that your professional opinion as an architectural engineer?"

"Yes it is," he replied confidently.

"That is all I wanted to hear!"

Samy had always expressed an interest in becoming an architect and a professional soccer player. The only thing he could not quite figure out was how to allocate his time between the two very different vocational objectives. He was, as always, confident that he would figure that out.

"Grandpa, do you remember when the Milwaukee engine said 'sold' on eBay?" Samy said thoughtfully.

"I sure do remember, you looked very worried at the time."

Samy wrinkled his nose for a moment, and said, "Santa probably did buy it there but there is no way to know for sure."

"Don't you think that is part of the 'magic' of Christmas?" I answered quickly.

"You are probably right Grandpa."

"However it got here it has found a good home on our layout. We will take good care of it and someday you will share it with your children and grandchildren. You can tell them the whole story." I was confident that someday he would do just that.

"By then we will have a lot of stories to tell, Grandpa."

Samy's use of the word "we" was not lost on me and I thought how very much I would like to be there. My confidence in my grandson told me in one way or another I would be. We had come a long way on our "journey" and it had taken us places we did not originally imagine. We had laughed at our mistakes, overcame the many obstacles we encountered, and had a great deal of fun doing so. Samy's excitement, enthusiasm, and confidence grew proportionately with our success.

§

Initially, our track plan was quite different. My young architect was responsible for adding a second level. Certain restrictions were in place in order for us to achieve the "must haves" on our layout. One of those was to have one train cross over the other at one place. We were quite confident that we would achieve all of our goals. After all, we had built a tremendous mountain range, constructed two tunnels, and added a second level of track! We had no way of knowing where our imaginations would take us next.

We watched as the Milwaukee climbed our new mountain track, enter and disappear into the tunnel, travel behind the site for our village, and gracefully speed past us on its way back to the mountain range.

Samy and I had built a mountain together. I knew this would be one of many mountains he will climb both now and in the future. He will conquer the many obstacles he may face as gracefully as that Milwaukee engine conquered our mountain pass. I want to be there to catch him if he falls, advise him should he ask, and provide him with love and support always. These are the "snapshots in time" we hold so dear and will remain in our hearts forever.

"The idea that no one is perfect is a view most commonly held by people with no grandchildren"

Doug Larson

CHAPTER 14

It Takes A Village

Time has a way of passing much faster than we would like. We both knew that we had to make a decision on the period in history we wanted our village to represent. Our journey thus far did not lead us to some distant area of America. Ironically, it led us to the very place we live. We toured the hardware store in the center of our town that has been in operation since 1900, and learned about its history as well. This inevitably opened the window for learning much about the history of our town and its historical landmarks.

A few days had passed since the Milwaukee engine made its first run through the upper mountain pass on our layout. I was cleaning up some wood scraps we had left that day when the telephone rang. I answered and the voice of my engineer said, "Grandpa, Mom said she will drop me off after school today and we can work on the trains."

"That's great, Samy, I will be looking forward to seeing you."

"I'll see you later, Grandpa."

"I'll be waiting for you, buddy," I said, thinking about how great it was to be so close to my grandson.

Before I knew it, the two of us were sitting in front of the computer deciding the type of architecture we wanted, and the time in history it represented. We had narrowed it down to two. We had "bookmarked" the web sites on the computer and had been back to them many times. This time was different because we were more motivated and we had taken a trip back in time to the exact time period in history we wanted our village to represent. You might say "this time it was personal."

Our walk through the historic downtown area where the hardware store is located made it easy to envision a "bustling hub" where farmers in the surrounding communities would bring their cotton. Crops, such as cotton, would then be shipped to the textile mills by train.

"The farmers must have really liked it when the railroad finally came," Samy commented.

"Before the train came to our town only small amounts of crops could be taken anywhere because the farmers were limited by how much they could fit in a wagon. Trips were often long and dangerous and not profitable."

We identified many of the historical homes and buildings that existed in our small town. Our favorite residential home, built in 1890, is one of only a few Queen Anne Victorian homes that remain today just as it did at the turn of the century. It is a small white clapboard house with a turret, and front porch loaded with an enormous amount of ornate moldings and architectural details. This home evokes memories of an era when our town was very small indeed. According to historical accounts, the magnolia trees that now dwarf the house and shade the porch were planted shortly after it was built. We had the privilege of walking past this house and can now appreciate why it is easy to picture the original owners as they sat on their gingerbread porch.

§

"Grandpa, can we build an exact duplicate of the hardware store?"

"Anything is possible Samy, but I think it would be very difficult especially if we wanted to match the surrounding buildings."

"Since it's such a special building, do you think anyone has already built a model of it?" Samy's question was a good one and had a great deal of merit.

"There's one way to find out. I am sure the store would be more than happy to help."

"Let's call the store and ask," Samy said.

We called the store and explained what we were doing and that we wanted a model of their store on our layout. They were extremely nice and said that given the history of the store they too would love to have a model but were sorry they could not help. We were somewhat disappointed but we had to be content with the fact that we had tried.

"Let's go to the site with the 'Americana' building kits and see if they make one just like the hardware store," I suggested.

§

We looked at the buildings and although they possessed the same architectural components, none was close enough to the size and shape of our hardware store. You see, "coming close" was not good enough. It was at this point we made the decision to stick to our original plan and include a post office, bakery, restaurant, drug store, school, church and log cabin on our layout. All that remained to do was to find our "period correct" buildings. We had not abandoned the idea of building a replica of our general merchandise or hardware store but decided to delay it until we had more experience building this type of scale model building. The log cabin we ordered specifically for the mountain range and the church was typical of those found in villages and towns in the early 1900s.

"I'd like the buildings to have cornices, arches above the windows, and lots of trim," Samy said.

"Where did you learn about cornices?" I said somewhat surprised.

"I think I read about them somewhere or heard Daddy talking about them," Samy replied in a very matter-of-fact manner.

I cannot say with any certainty that when I was seven years old the word "cornice" was part of my vocabulary, never mind know what it meant! The more time I spend with my grandson, the more amazed I am at what he is capable of saying and doing. He possesses that sense of wonder that seems to fade all too quickly as most people age. Only the very special among us seem to have the ability to retain that sense of wonder. He very often seems older than his years, but I am certain he is one of those "special" people that will have a profound effect on others in a very positive way

§

"Samy, it's "crunch" time" I announced.

"Crunch Time?" he asked.

"Yes it's time to decide and order these buildings before we are too old to build them."

"Can we order them today?" Samy asked with a great deal of excitement in his voice over the prospect of seeing the village we had planned become a reality.

"We sure can, I am as anxious as you are to see them on our layout."

We were on the site that offered the full line of late nineteenth century American commercial architectural buildings. They are typical of buildings found in business districts along railway lines and they remain today in small cities and rural towns across the United States. They featured tall narrow windows with decorative arched window heads and recessed front doorways common to this time period in our history. This beautiful and intricate style dominated building design beginning in the second half of the nineteenth century. The fact that Samy appreciated the details of commercial Victorian architecture made our selections even more exceptional.

"You do realize that these buildings are kits and we have to assemble them, put on the cornices, moldings over windows, paint the entire ornate trim, install the windows and even grout the brick!"

"That sounds like fun. I want to put the window trim and cornices on and paint."

"God bless you Samy, and your enthusiasm!"

We placed the houses in our "shopping cart," filled in the "ship to" and "bill to" portions of the online form and all that was left was the credit card information. I held out my hand and asked Samy "Which credit card are you going to use?" He immediately "slapped me five" and we put in the credit card number.

Our research was done and we finally placed our order for our village. We had come a long way and our further research just kept opening more doors and showing us that we were limited only by our imagination. Were we almost finished? Did we want to be? The answer to both questions was unquestionably no!

"How long do they take to get here?" Samy asked with a smile.

"They were all in stock, so probably two or three weeks."

"Really, It takes that long, Grandpa?"

"That will give us time to pick up the paint we will need and other supplies like glue and paint brushes."

"Samy, you do know that we made the right choice when it comes to the houses."

"I think they are so cool especially the details on them like the window trim and the cornices across the top."

§

"What time is your game tomorrow?" I asked.

"I think it's at 8 or 9 but I'm not sure."

Samy had been playing organized soccer since he was four and has exhibited a real natural talent for the game.

He has two athletic parents and a Father who played soccer through college. As far as I was concerned, it was clear to me that after watching him play I needed to take on a new hobby. I needed a camera and lens that would not miss a goal and would be able to zoom in from a distance. Since that day a few years back, I have prided myself in never missing one of his regular games. I wish I could say that about my photography!

"Do you remember the first soccer league you were in?" I asked with a smile.

"It was at the 'Y' and Mom and Dad were the coaches." Samy replied.

"You have to admit Samy, those early days of your soccer career were fun. The coaches you had were the best!"

"The coaches were the best, but you are forgetting something Grandpa," as he smiled and paused for a moment.

"What am I forgetting?"

"The photographer!" Samy said with a huge grin.

"Thanks for remembering the guy that took all those embarrassing photos of the little girls who looked to you for help and..."

"Oh Grandpa...!"

The league Samy was referring to was when Samy was four years old. It was a "mixed" league with boys and girls on the same team. I loved watching him play and I have many pictures of him helping the little girls on his team score a goal. I also have the "priceless" picture of a little girl with her arm around him and the look on his face was something to behold. I was sure that the day would be here much too quickly when such a photograph will evoke a much different response from my grandson. These "snapshots in time" are preserved digitally, but more importantly, they are the memories we will hold dear in our hearts forever.

§

Samy's skill level has increased dramatically and he is playing on "select" teams with players two years older than him. I have watched from the sidelines as Samy has done some incredibly difficult moves that I did not think were possible, particularly at my grandson's age. I have watched him in sub-freezing weather to incredibly hot, under beautifully sunny skies to pouring rain.

The photographic record that I have on a separate hard drive on my computer provides a digital record of these precious, priceless "snapshots in time" that I cherish. Our digital age leaves no excuse for parents and grandparents not to leave a large "digital footprint" to the next generation, especially when you consider the cost. How many times did my generation wish they had more pictures of themselves growing up and those of the most important people in their lives? I have assumed the role of self-appointed family historian. This is something I thoroughly enjoy, and that is as it should be!

A part of every grandparent clings to the memories of their grandchildren's early years. Perhaps that is because they too were younger and better able to "keep up" with them! I still "think" I am much younger than I am. I am determined to be there for Samy always. This generation of grandchildren has grandparents that are much "younger" than my parents and grandparents. The next generation of grandparents will be "younger" still.

Samy told me recently that he liked having me take pictures at his games. I told Samy that I enjoy watching him play and enjoy photographing his games. The most special part of the game to me is a soccer player named Samy! These "snapshots in time" are indeed priceless!

"Grandchildren are grandparent's link to the future, and grandparents are the child's link to the past"

UNKNOWN

CHAPTER 15

A Link To The Past

The voice we were listening to was coming out of that technological miracle called a transistor radio. The sports announcer for the New York Yankees, Mel Allen, was giving us the play by play of game five of the World Series. A group of us had gathered outside of school that sunny afternoon in October and listened as Don Larsen of the New York Yankees pitched the first perfect game in World Series history. The Yankees would go on to win the series over the Brooklyn Dodgers in the seventh game. Mickey Mantle hit 52 homeruns that year and finished with a .358 batting average. We couldn't have been happier, since in 1956, life was good and this just made it better.

I walked home from school that day with my best friend elated because our team had won and when we reached the street where we would go our separate ways, we agreed to meet soon at our "secret place" that we had discovered early last summer. We went home to change and drop off our school supplies. I was greeted at the door by my mother who always asked me how school was and what went on that day. I remember telling her about the Yankees and the first World Series perfect game and how we listened to it on my friend's transistor radio. I was old enough to realize that she would have liked it much better if I told her about my math class or how well I behaved in school that day, but she was wise enough to listen to me anyway.

The woods surrounded our development on all sides and since mine was among the first homes built, there were woods directly behind us as well. Exploring the thick woods fascinated us beyond measure. They seemed to never end and each time we stepped foot in them it was as if we were stepping into a page in the history books. Instantly, we became explorers mapping out and charting new territory. The stream that coiled through the woods was where we spent much of our time fishing. It provided us with a never ending source of adventure and mystery. To us it was like the Missouri and Mississippi Rivers were to Lewis and Clark. Although we were content with our part of the woods we vowed to someday explore further and follow our waterway as far as we could.

We met by a crudely built stone fireplace that day which someone had fashioned from rocks found along the stream. It was about two feet high and two feet wide and we saw an inscription in the side that read 1921! Thus far this had been our greatest treasure and we took great pride in knowing that we were the only ones who knew it was there.

The stream that ran through the woods fascinated us beyond measure the first day we laid eyes on it. We spent a considerable amount of time fishing "our" part of the stream. There were a few occasions when we followed it in search of a better fishing spot despite the many bends and turns it made. At one point the stream made a very sharp bend and disappeared from view. Stopping here always seemed like a good idea, but today was somehow different so we forged ahead. The banks of our waterway were becoming steeper as we progressed. The woods were becoming thicker and then suddenly the trail ended. We knew it was getting late and there wouldn't be much more light left, but we decided to go just a bit further.

The huge boulder we had climbed and were now standing on, gave us the view we were looking for. We could now see the direction the stream was taking from our new vantage point. Originally, we thought there were two streams that joined each other, split, and went in different directions. We now knew that might not be true. The stream made what looked like a huge backwards "C" as we looked through the dense woods downstream. We looked at each other and within a millisecond we both said "Where does it go?" Judging from the steep banks, thick woods, and lack of any trail at all, this was truly "undiscovered territory." We both knew we had discovered something special and we were determined to follow the stream as far as we could. The mystery and sense of adventure had us both excited and our imaginations ran wild with thoughts of what we were about to discover.

The temptation to go further that day seemed impossible to resist. We had always talked about following the "river" as far as we possibly could. Since the woods were growing thicker, our trail had all but disappeared, and the light was fading, we decided to turn back. Getting back the same way we came was much more difficult than we imagined.

§

Darkness was slowly enveloping the woods, which made it difficult to navigate the narrow, steep trail alongside the banks of our waterway. We broke thin branches every twenty-five yards or so to mark our trail. Had we done so on our initial excursion our journey home would have been much easier. Our speculation on what lay ahead ran wild. What would have happened if we had kept going? What might we have found? Did the river really make a turn back toward its original direction?

One thing we did know for sure was that we wanted to get home soon. Our parents would be worried and not very happy with us if we returned after dark. We were determined to get home swiftly and safely. The thick woods, lack of a clearly defined trail, the tall banks, and darkness were hampering our efforts to get back swiftly. The temperature had dropped slightly and the noise of the wind through the trees was unnerving. "No self-respecting explorer would let a little wind bother them" I thought to myself.

"How much further do you think we have to go?" My friend asked.

At this point there was no doubt that the two of us wished we had saved this expedition for another day allowing us more time. The only response that came to mind was "Too far and it's getting late."

Just then, the small clearing around our fireplace came into view. We were finally reaching our base camp and it never looked so good!

"Look just ahead on your right, there is the fireplace," and finally relief replaced anxiety.

Our excitement made us forget just how tired and hungry we were. Needless to say, it was good to be back in familiar territory and just in time! When we reached my friend's house, I hopped on my bike and rode home as quickly as possible. This was a ride we both had taken hundreds of times before, but this day was special. The events of the day crowded out thoughts of everything else. When my house was in view, my thoughts turned briefly to the early explorers and I remember thinking that this was probably how they might have felt when they reached their camp.

§

The sky was grey and cloudy the next morning and thoughts of our journey the afternoon before filled my mind while walking to school. My best friend and fellow explorer was waiting for me when the school parking lot came into view. He was usually the last one to get here this early, however today was different.

Throughout the morning and at lunch we talked about our plans for resuming our expedition as soon as we left school. We even drew a map together at lunchtime that showed the route we took and how we proposed to extend the trail we had previously taken. This was classified information we were not about to share with anyone until we had confirmed what lie ahead of what we were now calling Boulder Point.

The schoolroom clock seemed to move torturously slow all day. The seconds seemed like minutes and the minutes like hours. If that wasn't bad enough, about fifteen minutes before we were about to be dismissed we heard a loud clap of thunder followed by a torrential downpour. It was raining so hard our teacher began to close and lock all the windows. The windows were the type you needed a long pole designed to pull the upper windows shut. I grabbed the pole for our teacher and my friend helped finish closing the windows.

The two of us just stood next to those huge windows in total disbelief. This could not be happening on the day we were about to make an amazing discovery! We were so engrossed in what was happening outside that neither of us heeded the bell for dismissal. We gazed out the windows and just stood there looking very disillusioned.

The standard procedure on days when it rained or snowed, was one of our mothers would pick us up and drive us home. Our teacher thanked us for our help with the windows and gently reminded us to get in line with our class. We followed our class down the hallway to the exterior doors which led to the parking lot.

As we climbed into the car to get out of the pouring rain, we were greeted by my best friend's mother. We were not aware that the look on our faces was as obvious as it must have been. We had learned on a number of occasions that there wasn't much you could hide from our mothers!

"What is the matter with the two of you? I'd say you look like you lost your best friend but the two of you are right here."

"It's just the rain that's all," we replied.

"It's supposed to rain for the rest of the week," she continued.

That was definitely not what either of us wanted to hear, especially not on this particular day. Our conversation on the ride home was about how long this school day seemed to take and how the hours passed so slowly.

"It was like torture looking at that clock. The minutes seemed like hours."

"If you think that was torture can you imagine if my mom is right and it rains all week?"

We pulled up to my house and I saw my mother standing at the door waving to us. I got out of the car, said thank you for the ride home, and ran to the door. Now it was raining even harder!

"How was your day?" my mom asked.

This all seemed like some kind of conspiracy. Was my mom part of it? I tried my best to tell my mom about what we did in math, history and how we heard the thunder and helped close the windows. I felt guilty about the "helping close the window part" even though I have helped do it many times before.

§

Watching the weather report on the local news was not something I had done often, with the possible exception of winter storm warnings for snow and school closings. We both watched the weather reports and shared what we had learned at school each day. The conclusion we came to was that it was quite possibly never going to stop raining! Our eagerness to resume our exploration increased exponentially with each passing day. This was just a temporary setback that gave us more time to plan and make a list of supplies we would bring with us. Our anticipation was heightened each day by the very thought of resuming our expedition into new and unexplored territory.

That Friday afternoon the sun broke through the clouds and we were extremely happy. Watching the weather gave us an idea of what we could expect when we reached the stream. Widespread flooding was prevalent in some areas and was responsible for the closing of the small two-lane road that crossed over our waterway on Thursday. Even though we were armed with this knowledge, we were not quite prepared for what we were about to see when we reached the small clearing that surrounded our cherished fireplace.

The fireplace, which served as our "base camp" was located approximately fifty yards from the stream that had fascinated us for so long. The mud grew thicker with each step we took and when we reached the fireplace, we easily saw why. The banks of the stream were not visible and the water had crept up at least twenty feet on either side of the stream. The path the stream had made when the water was at its highest point was clearly visible. Tall grass, that grew on each side of our waterway, bent to the ground by the force of the water, was slowly reacting to the warm rays of the sun as it filtered through the trees.

We quickly estimated that even though it was receding, it presently was six feet deep and sixty to seventy feet wide! We knew we would not be able to resume our exploration any time soon. We would have to wait until our waterway returned to normal levels. The sheer size and depth of the stream was amazing and for the moment diverted our attention. We walked up to the small two-lane road that made a sharp turn on to a bridge over the stream. The waterline on the bridge was over the top of the cement and stone that composed its sides.

"Can you imagine if the stream was always this size?" I said.

"We would need a boat to cross and it probably wouldn't be as shallow in the summer," my friend answered.

§

It was not until the middle of the following week that we ventured back to our base camp. The water had receded however; the depth and speed of the water amazed both of us. A short distance away from where we were standing, we heard the sound of rushing water so we went to investigate. The storm had dislodged a few large boulders and they came to rest almost in a straight line across the water. The sound that we heard was the sound of the water cascading over these new stone additions to or waterway. There now was a waterfall where previously there had been none! As the water fell into the lower level, we noticed that the riverbed had been disturbed significantly. The cascading water formed a deep pool the size of a small pond before exiting downstream.

"What a great place this will be for fishing!" I said excitedly.

"This looks so cool. I do not believe how things have changed," my friend said.

"Just when we thought we had discovered the best place in the world, it gets even better."

We could not possibly have known what was in store for us when we were able to resume our journey. During the next two weeks, we returned several times to check on the level of the stream and the muddy conditions that were preventing us from resuming our exploration. The weather remained sunny for much of this time and we were confident that we could complete our journey very soon. We used this time to revise our map and store some supplies like a rope and some flashlights. This was quite possibly the most exciting thing to happen to us in a very long time. The anticipation we felt was growing with each passing day!

§

It was a clear sunny Saturday morning and we set out for our base camp very early. We looked forward to this day for what seemed like months. As we walked down toward the stream and the adjacent trail, we noticed that the stream was still higher than normal. We walked along the trail noting any differences the storm may have made. The waterfall looked as though it had been there forever. The small pond below appeared to have become larger. Boulder Point was just ahead and we wasted no time climbing to the top. The top of Boulder Point gave us the advantage of mapping out the route we would take. Climbing down the opposite side of the boulder was much easier since there were other large stones arranged in almost a "step-like" fashion. The next part of our adventure proved to be the most demanding, since we no longer had the luxury of a trail. The only trail we had was the one we were making. We threaded our way carefully through the woods following the route the stream was taking us. It was only after we had traveled about fifty yards or so that we realized our waterway did make what we had referred to as a backwards "C". The stream headed back in the direction we had always thought it took. It was only after we traveled a short distance further that we saw something we never expected to see. A huge oak tree, at least six to seven feet in diameter had fallen across the stream. When we reached the tree, we could see an island the stream ran around.

It looked like the tree had fallen quite some time ago. The huge base of the tree towered over us when we stood next to it. The island was quite large and had a number of tall trees on it. Small pebbles covered the "beaches" of the island and completely encircled it. This enormous tree that spanned the entire distance in front of the island, afforded us easy access to the beach. We wasted no time climbing up to our bridge and walked out to the center of the stream. The two of us sat down on the tree in front of our island and marveled at what we had "discovered".

"This is unbelievable! It's like something you would see in National Geographic!"

"Never in a million years did I think we would find something this cool."

After jumping quickly on to the island beach, I remember saying to my friend "Come on what are you waiting for?"

"I was thinking about what we could name our island," he responded.

Looking back, there is no doubt that we were stunned, excited, and mesmerized by what we had discovered.

The island was oval-shaped and at its longest point was about fifty feet and its widest point was twenty to twenty-five feet. We explored every square inch of the island that day. The entire island was elevated and its beaches sloped gently toward the rushing water. The banks of the stream looked to be about three feet high on the sides of the island, giving it protection from the stream as it rushed by. We were ecstatic about our find and decided to name the island "Cucamonga Island." The beaches, especially the largest one closest to our tree we named "Pebble Beach". The tree we called "Cucamonga Bridge".

We decided our island needed much more exploration and we were not going to announce our discovery to anyone.

§

"Hey you two, where are you? Didn't you hear us calling you?"

Samy and I had become so engrossed in the story that we lost track of time and apparently did not hear a thing.

"We are under here, Mom," Samy said peering out from under the train table.

"So that's where you two have been for so long."

"Grandpa just finished telling me this really cool story about when he was young."

"There's more to that story but it will have to wait, buddy." I was very happy we were able to complete most of the story and that Samy found it as exciting as he did! We had gone back in time together to relive a time in the 1950s when I was just about Samy's age. We did not need a plutonium-powered DeLorean or a flux capacitor to do it!

I could not help but think that although our world has changed dramatically in so many ways, some things stay the same. More people should look at the world through the lens of an eight year old. This is but one "snapshot in time" we shared together and we will cherish forever!

"They say genes tend to skip generations. Maybe that's why grandparents find their grandchildren so likeable."

Joan McIntosh

CHAPTER 16

Sense of Wonder and Humor

"Anticipation is half the fun" is an expression that many of us have heard quite often. Too often the desire to have things "right now" takes precedence over what could be the pride we feel when we are patient and savor those moments when we not only were patient, but persevered in what we were doing. To be able to look forward to something is important in all aspects of our lives and at any age. Wanting everything "now" and not working for it is not! The development of personal responsibility and knowing that our actions and decisions we make today do have consequences are important concepts for us all.

Sometimes the going gets tough and success at whatever we are doing seems light years away. This is when many become discouraged and give up. Confidence often comes with success and our success requires us to be patient and persistent. I knew Samy was fully aware of the value of "patience and perseverance". This was something instilled in him at a very early age.

"Grandpa, when will our buildings be here?" Samy asked.

"The Americana buildings we ordered would be here in two to three weeks." I responded, looking for signs of disappointment on Samy's face. There were none.

We purchased the necessary paint, brushes, and glue we needed to complete our buildings and were anxiously awaiting their arrival. During that time, we made the necessary preparations and planned the exact location of each of our buildings. Since we now had an elevated track, our village would have railroad siding behind the stores as well as an elevated mountain pass in the background. We made provision for a country road beyond the tracks in the rear of our buildings. The buildings we ordered were by far the most realistic and detailed we had seen, and we researched many types of buildings. They did not come with lights inside, so Samy and I purchased lights and did the preliminary wiring underneath our layout.

§

"Grandpa, how do the lights get the electricity to light up?"

"Our main power strip receives the electricity from the wall. The transformer converts it to a much lower voltage, which sends the electricity through the wires we connect to our main circuit board. It is then sent through the wires that are connected to the lights."

"Is it just like the wires to the track?" Samy asked.

"The only difference is the electricity provided to the track increases or decreases when you raise or lower the lever on the transformer."

"How do we stop the lights from getting lower or higher?"

"Good question, I have something to show you."

"This is the circuit board that will keep the voltage constant so the lights won't dim." Samy's interest piqued as we both examined the circuit board and its terminals.

"That looks like something we took out of your old computer when we took it apart that time."

"Very good Samy, you are not far off. The printed circuits on this board are very similar to some in the computer. This one has twelve terminals to connect wires. When they are connected they maintain a constant voltage to whatever is connected to them."

"You mean so the lights will all have the same amount of electricity all the time and won't go higher and lower?"

"Exactly, I couldn't have said it better. This device will act like the brain of our layout regulating the electrical flow of not only our building lights but also all other accessories. We are going to wire switches and place them on our control panel just like the wall switches in a house."

"Will the switches that we bought control the lights?" Samy asked.

"They will control the building lights, street lights, log cabin, the yard lights, and anything else we want. We can wire them so we have a switch for each house or one for a group of houses."

"That's going to be so cool, Grandpa, but I don't think we will need a switch for every single one."

"Probably not, I was thinking one for all the stores, one for the church, log cabin, and yard lights, and then add more as we grow. We are definitely getting there Samy, and considering all we have added since our original plan we are doing quite well," I said with a certain amount of satisfaction in my voice.

"Grandpa, don't forget the waterfalls and anything else we might add," Samy, said showing off those dimples I love so much.

"I remember our discussion about the waterfalls we wanted to incorporate into our layout. We had even made a provision for them when we designed our mountain and mountain streams. As far as your reminder is concerned, they go under the heading of future projects...way into the future."

"We will definitely have to build a time machine now to go in to the future to get them."

"Samy you are definitely...too much." I responded chuckling at Samy's last comment.

§

The previous year I was about to discard a very old computer when my inquisitive grandson said, "What's inside, Grandpa?" It was not long before we had the outer casing off, had removed the motherboard, memory, sound card, video card, and hard drive and discussed the function of each. Our dissection of a computer that was to be discarded or donated for parts became a project that proved to be quite an educational experience for Samy.

"You know Grandpa, I always wondered what was inside of the computer and now I know!"

"Keep this in mind Samy, computers did not exist when your Mom and Dad were your age, and were not even a thought when I was your age."

"Was the light bulb invented when you were my age, Grandpa?" Samy said as he tried to but was unsuccessful at holding back his laughter.

"O.K. Samy...I will remember that!" Samy had definitely caught me off guard with his last question and his timing was impeccable.

"What about cars..., the telephone and..."

"Now you're pushing it buddy!" I replied as we both broke into laughter at Samy's last remark.

§

Samy's sense of humor was growing with his personality and character and he is always a pleasure to work with or be involved with in any way. I had to remind myself that he was eight years old. It was quite remarkable that he was interested in taking apart an old computer and identifying the function of the parts, in addition to understanding the power grid of our layout.

We could have just purchased illuminated toy houses, streetlights, and accessories. We were genuinely interested in the authenticity and realism of our project and we wanted to create something as realistic as possible. Samy was now interested in the electrical concepts as well. This interest, together with our research into the history of the period made our project so much more special. Samy's involvement in our project would make it much more of a learning experience and a memorable one as well. Nothing will ever be more special to me than creating these memories together, except the creation of future memories.

"Where are we going to put the stores we bought, Grandpa?"

"I would say we put them across the back facing the front of the layout. What do you think?"

"I think that is a good idea because that way they could have the train deliver supplies on the lower level right to their back door," Samy said as if the logic of his answer was common sense.

"The upper level would be in the background, with its rock walls and shrubs for quite a spectacular backdrop," I added.

"We could also put our trestle bridge on the upper level." Samy said excitedly.

"Samy, if you can imagine it you..."

"I know Grandpa... you can do it!"

§

Samy remained quite busy between school and soccer. On the weekends, I would be there taking pictures at his games. Samy was becoming better with each game. His skill level had increased dramatically in the span of only a couple of years. The photographs, in my view, showed his dimples replaced by determination and his cute walk replaced by some very fancy footwork. My new photography hobby was more enjoyable than expected. Of course, I could not think of a better subject to photograph.

I was learning to capture images I previously thought only a professional photographer could. I surprised myself more with each game and marveled at what one could achieve with the right equipment. To be able to stand anywhere on the sidelines and capture those moments during a soccer game was truly a labor of love for me. I especially enjoyed being able to capture those moments that highlighted sportsmanship and celebration.

Many years ago when I took pictures of my own children on different occasions, we took 12-24 pictures, waited to have them developed and hoped for the best. The digital age has now made it possible for me to take crystal clear action photos from anywhere on the field. I was averaging hundreds of photos or more per game, saved to a disc, labeled and preserved for the day when Samy and his parents can look back and remember. Perhaps they too will refer to this as a "simpler time" when life was more basic.

§

I am honored to be part of creating these special memories with Samy. He is happy to be part of them! Quite literally, these "snapshots in time" would digitally record these precious moments forever.

"Yesterday is history. Tomorrow is a mystery. Today is a gift. That's why we call it the present."
BILL KEANE

CHAPTER 17

𝔄 𝔙𝔦𝔰𝔦𝔱 𝔗𝔬 𝔗𝔥𝔢 𝔉𝔲𝔱𝔲𝔯𝔢

We had all the comforts of home including electricity with a power strip located on the beams that surrounded us, lighting, pillows, and all the supplies we felt were necessary. The sense of security our structure provided by its heavy beams and vertical supports would make anyone feel as if they were in a highly classified and very secure structure. This was a world controlled only by our collective imaginations. This was truly a special place for members only. The sign posted on the door to the room read "Danger: Restricted Area". We met here that day to discuss additional plans for our train layout.

§

Samy looked up at the writing on one of the center beams that read "Samy & Grandpa 2010". He gave me that impish smile that showed his dimples so well, and laughed saying, "Did they have magic markers when you were my age Grandpa?"

"No Samy, we had to be content with writing on the walls of our cave using dye we made from plant roots," I said just before I launched my "tickle attack" on him.

We both were laughing when we heard the doorbell ring. Could that bell be announcing the much-anticipated arrival of our village? We went downstairs quickly to check. There was a package sitting on the front porch addressed to Grandma, and judging by its size, we knew that it was much too small to be our village. We checked the package to confirm that it was not our village. Although we were slightly disappointed, we really did not expect to receive our buildings that day.

"I have an idea Samy, just follow me," I said mysteriously.

"Where are we going?" Samy replied curiously.

"We are going to get on the computer and type in the tracking number they gave us when we ordered the buildings."

"What will that do, Grandpa?"

"It should tell us exactly where our package is, even if it's in some remote region of the country."

We typed in the tracking numbers and that brought up a screen, which showed us all the cities it had stopped and where it was now. Samy's eyes did not leave the screen as I pointed out where it had been and where it was now. Samy pointed out its last stop was in Stallings, a town that was very close to us.

"Do you think it will come today, Grandpa?"

"I'm not sure because usually they are marked 'Out for Delivery' if they are coming that day."

"We wouldn't really have time to work on them if they came today anyway since it is getting late."

We went back to our conference room and I followed Samy as he led me to what had become our clubhouse, media center, and very special place. He looked at me and said, quite unexpectedly, "How old is "Old Bob now?"

"He just celebrated his sixty-first birthday and he is still going strong. Why do you ask, Samy?"

"I wonder what it will be like sixty-one years from now."

"You know that I have always told you that the past can sometimes act as a window to the future. Let us take a trip to the future to when you are about my age. The flux capacitor is broken so we'll have to use our imagination."

"A trip sounds good to me, Grandpa," Samy responded enthusiastically. Samy had learned that our journey together was about "expecting the unexpected" and he as well as I loved every twist and turn our journey presented us.

"Buckle up and get ready for our trip," I said.

"I'm ready Grandpa," Samy replied with a great deal of enthusiasm in his voice

§

The year is 2052. You live with your wife and two children in a house that is composed of a space-age alloy because wood is no longer used. This alloy is stronger than steel and completely weather and insect proof. Your furniture is made of blocks or pyramids of different colored foam rubber that is safe for everyone.

"A wife...two kids? R e a l l y Grandpa," Samy chuckled.

I knew the day was approaching when his response may be somewhat different when it came to the opposite sex. I was very comfortable to wait until that day came.

"Maybe three kids," I replied.

There are several dials on the walls of your house in each room. This particular day is a very dreary one and it is raining.

"I forgot to ask, what is your wife's name?"

"OH Grandpa...Yuk!"

Since it is a very dreary day, you get up and turn the dial to "S" for sunlight. The room you are in will glow just as if you were standing outside in the sun. Of course, this is powered by a solar array you have on your reflective roof. You hear your ten-year-old son say to his mother as he is about to take his sonic shower, "Can I throw these jeans away?"

"How long have you worn them?" his mother asks. "A week," he says.

"Yes, by all means, throw them away."

So into the wastebasket go his disposable jeans. However, before he goes to bed he decides a light snack would be a super idea. A vitamin burger made from all organic foods and supplements with a glass of organic milk sound good. Inside the cabinet over the sink in a carton is a "sandwich" wrapped in special paper. Around the paper is a throwaway cord. He plugs in the cord and ten seconds later he has a well-cooked, piping hot snack. Before getting into bed he checks the solar clock that he had "wound" that day by placing it in the sun four a couple of hours. It will now run for a month.

The next day he wakes up to the sound of the vacuum cleaner, which is traveling throughout the house cleaning all the floors. His mother had pushed a button above her bed that signaled the vacuum to come out of the wall and begin the cleaning cycle. The next button mom pushes is the one that starts the coffee perking and breakfast cooking.

"This sounds cool but really Grandpa, do you think it will be like that?"

"Think back to when your mother was young. Did anyone think they would have a computer, microwave, or the internet?"

"What else could we have?" Samy asked.

"Instead of the plug-in sandwich he might have a food replicator."

"What is a food replicator, Grandpa?"

"Here's how it works, you walk up to a device that has been built into the wall and simply say 'Coffee black' and a cup of black coffee will materialize before your very eyes in the appropriate cup or you might say 'I'd like a banana smoothie' and the same thing will happen. On the other hand, you might be in the mood for some 'Klignon blood worms', and a delicious plate of Klignon blood worms will materialize before your very eyes."

"You know what I think, Grandpa?"

"I probably do, but tell me anyway, Samy."

"I think you have been watching too much Star Trek," he said mischievously, with those big dimples showing.

"Speaking about Star Trek, can you imagine a day when you are able to step into a device and have all the molecules in your body scrambled and transported a long distance away, then instantly unscrambled at your destination? There will be no need to get in the car, train, or airplane. Long hours on the highway will be outdated. Can you imagine when we take our summer family vacation to the beach and are able to get there in seconds?"

"Now I know you have been watching too much Star Trek!"

"The key word here Samy is imagine," I replied.

"There are some things we can imagine that will never come true. Everything we imagine doesn't come true," Samy said, only this time more thoughtfully.

"You are absolutely right, but that is where it starts. Then we apply all we know whether it be math, physics, biology, engineering or anything else necessary to make it happen."

Samy seemed surprised by my response at first then paused thoughtfully and said, "I think I know what you mean, Grandpa."

§

I knew this sounded like something from a Hollywood science fiction movie to Samy, but I also knew Samy was starting to think about the possibilities. We talked more about possible future inventions and how they would change, the way people live. I was very proud to hear Samy's thoughts about future inventions and their impact on our lives.

"Let's just say we could do all that, couldn't we help feed people who have no food, or find cures for sick people?"

"We could and I do believe someday we will, but that will be up to you. You should be proud of yourself for thinking of helping people less fortunate than you."

We talked for an hour about the times when people would have thought you were crazy if you said someday hundreds of people would board an airplane together and fly thousands of miles away. If you described cell phones to people just 50 years ago, they probably would not believe you. Can you imagine the reaction you would receive if in 1940 you told someone the United States would land a man on the moon? Yesterday's science fiction often becomes today's reality.

§

"Grandpa," Samy said holding up his right hand placing his thumb against the palm of his hand and formed a 'V' by keeping his remaining fingers split "Live long and prosper."

I did the same and said that if he was not careful the Vulcan mind meld was next. We laughed a lot together that day, and I could not imagine a world without Samy in it! He is destined to have an impact on it, and he is the reason I am optimistic about the future! These "snapshots in time" will indeed influence the course of events yet to come and are priceless on so many levels.

"Imagination is the beginning of creation. You imagine what you desire, you will what you imagine, and at last you create what you will."

GEORGE BERNARD SHAW

CHAPTER 18

𝕬ttention 𝕿o 𝕯etail

𝕴magination is the key to many things. Many of us have difficulty imagining the joy even a simple cardboard box can bring. When we are very young, a cardboard box can provide many hours of pure enjoyment. Children may use it as a house and carve windows in it, others may stack several boxes in an attempt to recreate buildings and in this regard the "sky is the limit." To Samy and me, cardboard boxes represented presents dropped off by a delivery service. Subconsciously, it was Christmas morning every time a delivery we were waiting for arrived.

It was very late in the day when the doorbell rang and I heard the sound of a truck pulling away. I looked out the front door and saw the package we had been expecting for quite some time, sitting on the front porch. The container was much larger than I expected. The word "Fragile" was stamped on all sides of the box so I was extremely careful bringing it through the front door. Once upstairs, I decided to give my partner a call. Since it was almost 8 PM, I decided to wait until tomorrow, which was Saturday, and Samy did not have a soccer game scheduled.

Early Saturday morning I gave Samy a call to tell him that our village had arrived. His enthusiasm and excitement were always contagious and today was no different. He asked his mother if he could go to my house because our village had arrived.

"Mom said she will take me in fifteen minutes," he said with his typical excitement and enthusiasm.

"I'll be waiting for you."

"Do they look as realistic as they did in the pictures?" Samy asked.

"I have not opened the box yet. I wanted to wait for you," I said, knowing that Samy loved to open each package we ordered as if Santa left them on Christmas morning.

"Thanks, Grandpa, I'll be there in a few minutes."

Samy seemed grateful that the "grand opening" of the boxes had not taken place without him. This was what I have learned to expect from him. I did not want to miss the look on my grandson's face when we opened those boxes!

§

Ten minutes after I hung up the phone, I heard Samy coming up the stairs. I was in the train room next to a card table we had set up and covered for the express purpose of assembling and painting our buildings. We were very careful about covering the floor and the table itself with cardboard since we knew working with paint and glue could get messy. When he entered the room he was immediately surprised with the size of the box our village was delivered in.

"Wow, I don't believe the size of that box, it's humongous!" Samy exclaimed as he walked quickly over to it.

"I think it is time for the grand opening, what do you think?"

"I can't wait to see if the buildings look as good as they did in the pictures," Samy said excitedly.

"Remember Samy, the pictures showed the buildings after they were assembled, painted, grouted, and aged," I cautioned my grandson.

We opened the large cardboard outer container from the bottom by carefully cutting the packing tape that held our treasure together. We slid off the outer box and we both said how impressed we were by the amount of packing material inside. We found each individual box protected by packing material that could withstand even the most serious blow that might happen in shipping. We took out each box and placed it under the table until the entire box was empty.

"O.K. Samy, which building would you like to see first?" I was just as anxious as Samy was to see our village.

"Let's open the drug store because that has the same architecture as the restaurant, bakery and post office."

"Great idea Samy," I said as I handed him the box with the picture of our drugstore on it.

Samy carefully opened the box as if it contained some irreplaceable treasure. In many ways, it was to us and we were determined to make every effort to do this correctly. The box was only about three inches high and we knew the house was closer to seven inches when assembled. When he finished opening the box, he looked up and said, "After we look at all the pieces let's put everything back in each box so we don't lose anything, O.K. Grandpa?"

"Good idea, because there is no way we will be finished gluing them together today."

Samy carefully took out the front, back, and sides of the drug store and held them together. We put a small piece of masking tape on the back and front of each sidewall to hold them together so we could get the full effect of our turn-of-the-century drug store. Samy balanced the cornice that ran across the top of the building and we now were admiring our first building. We stood the cover of the box next to our building to compare it with the picture.

"Well, what do you think?" I asked Samy.

"I think the brick is redder than the picture but everything else is great!" Samy had a very analytical look on his face as he continued to examine our building. Samy reminded me of an architect examining a blueprint.

"Don't worry about the brick, when we grout the lines in between the bricks we will be aging it also."

"Do you mean we will be lightening the color?" Samy asked.

"Yes exactly, just as the years and weather age brick to some degree, we will be aging it as well. Don't forget we have that special spray that makes the plastic look like aged brick."

"Look at the details on the cornice, Grandpa, and the ornate trim around the windows! When we are finished with the painting, grouting, and aging they will look even better than the pictures on the boxes," Samy stated with a great deal of confidence.

"It sure looks like we made the right choice in buildings and your evaluation of how they will look when we are finished is correct," I answered.

"We sure did. I did not think they were going to be as detailed as they are. The tall narrow windows, cornices and the storefronts have recessed doorways just like the hardware store in town." Samy continued commenting on the details of the building and he spoke with a combination of authority and excitement.

"We have managed to be historically accurate, true to scale, and appropriate for this time period in American history."

We did the same for each of our buildings and we commented on how each of the buildings had their own unique charm even though the architecture was similar. We were also very impressed with the thickness of the outer walls. This thickness would make our buildings easier to work with and easier to glue perfectly square.

The school, log cabin, and church were different from our commercial buildings. We came to the conclusion that these buildings should be different. We took out the supplies we purchased such as the two different types of glue, various historical paint colors, and the roofs for each building.

"What should we do first, Grandpa? Should we read the directions?"

"You read them to me and I will compare them to the plan we developed. They may have some helpful tips that we haven't thought of."

§

I watched Samy as he read the directions for the assembly of the drug store and remembered thinking how different life would be without him. He was a constant source of joy in a world full of uncertainty. He found wonder in collecting seashells at the beach, flying a kite, or digging in the sand. I loved how we would go out for breakfast after church on Sundays. We shared many memories in the backseat of the car when Mom and Dad would stop for groceries and Samy would insist that we remain in the car. He did this so I could tell him stories as had become our custom over the last few years. There was much laughter shared in that backseat, and neither of us was anxious for Mom and Dad to come out of the supermarket. The only time we seemed to get out of the car now was when we stopped at the local sporting goods store where they had a putting green inside. We made good use of that putting green over the years!

"Grandpa, were you listening?" I laughed and told Samy what I was thinking about only toward the end of his reading. I then asked Samy if we should write a book and call it "Backseat".

"You should, Grandpa. That would be so cool."

"How would I do that?"

I had the distinct impression that Samy already knew what I was up to. My grandson immediately answered, "By using your imagination, Grandpa!"

"Just because I imagine it that doesn't...." Samy inter-rupted by saying. "Oh Grandpa...!"

I was happy to see that Samy had not forgotten our previous discussion.

§

We decided after unpacking all of the buildings that we would pick out the colors for each building. The glue that we purchased was the same glue that I had used as a young boy when I assembled my models of destroyers and aircraft car-riers. The very odor of the glue made it seem like yesterday.

I explained to Samy that the glue had the effect of "melt-ing" the plastic so the pieces were very strong once dried. You had to be very precise when lining up the sides of the buildings to insure they would be perfectly square. They had flat roofs that fit inside the exterior walls so we decided that would be a good way to make sure the buildings remained square and all pieces would fit. The time went by quickly and we realized that since we were going out to dinner that night it would not be a good idea to rush. We remembered, as always, "It's the journey not the destination."

"Nothing is so contagious as enthusiasm."

SAMUEL TAYLOR COLERIDGE

CHAPTER 19

Enthusiasm "Is" Contagious

Samy's enthusiasm and sense of wonder were no doubt contagious. They provided much of the motivation needed during our journey together. His willingness to do whatever was necessary to make our journey a success was inspiring. Samy's contributions to our journey and his suggestions were nothing short of amazing.

I could not help but think the enthusiasm that Samy displayed on every occasion came from his seemingly never-ending sense of wonder about the world around him. Where did it come from? What was the source? We must find a way to "tap in" to the source of such an extraordinary and imaginative power. Our journey together was the vehicle that would allow us to share the amazing and wonderful phenomenon we were now experiencing. What started out as the creation of a model railroad had become so much more.

The details of the buildings we received were truly remarkable. Perhaps it was this along with the fact that we wanted our plans to proceed smoothly that directed us to do what we did next. Whatever the reasons were, we made our decision and there was no turning back.

§

There was a slight groove on the edge of the front and back walls. The sidewalls fit into these grooves with no margin for error. The glue would attach them permanently. This part was irreversible, so together we designed a "box" from scrap pieces of lumber that along with the roof would hold our buildings "square" until the glue dried. We literally made a "dry run" lining up the back and sides of the building, and then positioned the roof in the correct place. When we were convinced it was foolproof, we complimented ourselves and began to assemble our first building, our drug store.

The odor of the glue reminded me of my model-building days as a young boy. Surely, no one should miss the opportunity to put a model together. I will never forget this "rite of passage" and I was honored to have the privilege of sharing a similar experience with my grandson. Samy and I had already built several different types of aircraft, which he prominently displayed in his room. Dad hung them skillfully from the ceiling with fishing line and the whole fleet protected him.

I remembered, as though it were yesterday, the model battleships, aircraft carriers, and destroyers I built when I was just slightly older than Samy. The smell of the glue we used in building our village made me marvel at the sensory memory the glue we were using activated. Better still, the glue used then was the exact same plastic cement we were using now.

We ran a very small amount of glue in the channel provided on both sides of the back of the building and quickly stood the sides up even with the edges. After thirty seconds, I turned it upside down with the roof and our "square invention" in place. We repeated the gluing procedure and everything appeared to be lining up, as it should. The edges lined up perfectly and when we returned the building to its upright position, everything looked great! We then took out our carpenters square and placed it at each corner. The building was indeed square and the roof fit perfectly!

The next morning we checked on the strength of the building. We also checked for gaps that may appear in the corners. They looked great except in one place on the inside of one of the corners. This was especially important so no light would shine through when we illuminated our buildings. We had purchased a type of glue for the gaps the instructions said are inevitable. The buildings were as strong as the commercial brick Victorian buildings they represented!

§

A few days had passed before we had another opportunity to work on our buildings. Samy came over that day and was his usual enthusiastic self. I showed him the drug store that we glued, the custom made square, and the glue we needed. He examined the building and the tool we had made to keep the building square as the glue dried. We discussed how this particular glue worked and how the plastic actually melted somewhat at the point of contact. Gloves and safety glasses were necessary. Proper ventilation for the glue we were about to use was also. We opened the windows before we started, and put on our safety glasses and gloves. We lined up all of our tools and materials and did our customary dry run to make sure everything lined up square.

Samy seemed fascinated by the square tool we had made to hold the parts of the buildings in place while the glue dried.

"Grandpa this wood square we made sure looks like it makes things easier for keeping the walls of the buildings in place. It reminds me of when they put a temporary beam across a ceiling and then put in a stronger one."

"Did you see that on a television show?" I asked.

"No I remember Daddy doing that on one of the houses we remodeled," he said authoritatively.

"It's a similar concept, holding something in place while you work to make sure everything is secure," I added.

"Grandpa, we should put the wood square around the building first and then put a couple of those 2 x 4 blocks inside, line up the walls and then put on the glue."

"That's an even better idea, now the walls will be supported on two sides leaving our hands free to make minor adjustments," I said approvingly at Samy's improvement to our already effective tool. This kind of creative thinking, or "inventiveness," will only show itself when given the opportunity to do so. This activity was tailor-made for such skills.

Samy slipped the wood square around the building, placed two blocks of wood inside and I ran a small amount of glue in the channel provided. The sides and back worked perfectly and we found that as the glue dried we could slide our invention toward the top and repeat the procedure.

We turned the building upside down sliding the wood square downward and repeated the gluing of the sidewalls to the front of the building. Sammy checked the corners of each, both inside and out, with the small metal carpenters square and everything checked out perfectly. We carefully followed the same procedure for buildings three and four and within an hour, we had successfully completed the most critical part of our buildings!

"This is even more fun than I thought it would be, Grandpa," Samy said as we stepped back to admire our work.

"That's because we make a great team and we were prepared. We didn't just rush into it without a plan and start gluing."

"What's next?" Samy asked with his usual enthusiastic tone.

"Next we take a nap." I responded.

"Oh ...Grandpa, really what should we do next?"

"We should let them dry for an hour or so. Then we should grout the lines in the brick so they look like real mortar and it will tone down the red and give the brick the 'aged' look we want."

"What do we use to grout the lines in the brick so it looks like mortar?" Samy said with a very serious look on his face.

"The instructions say to use paint and then wipe it off with a smooth sponge, but I am not so sure about that."

"How about using spackle, Grandpa?" Samy replied without hesitation.

"That's a great idea, because more of it will stay where we want it and less where we don't! Another benefit of using spackle will be the "aged" look it will give the brick if it should dry with a haze over the brick."

§

Mortaring the thin lines of the buildings proved to be quite a challenge. We quickly realized that if we applied our "mortar" to the buildings and allowed it to dry for a few minutes the small amount that remained on the brick after wiping the walls provided the aged look we wanted to achieve. We spackled our buildings that day for hours but they were coming out so good we were unaware just how much time had passed. The "mortar" we were putting on the buildings really gave them the weathered look of the one hundred plus year old buildings we saw in our research and had visited in our own town.

The aging liquid we had applied to the exterior toned down the smooth plastic look and our buildings really were starting to come to life. They truly looked as though they had stepped off the pages of a history book! The very fine lines in the buildings where our mortar went proved to be challenging, but extremely realistic when complete.

By this time both of us looked like we had spackled a room. We did manage to keep our work neat however, our clothes told another story. I looked over at my part-ner and said, "It looks like you missed a spot, Samy!"

"What spot did I miss?" He asked as he examined his work looking for the missed spot.

"This one," I said as I placed a dab of spackle on the tip of his nose.

Samy reciprocated and just as I received my ceremo-nial dab of spackle, we heard the sound of Grandma's voice asking us to come down to have something to eat. We decided we were appropriately spackled to go down-stairs to greet Grandma. As we entered the kitchen, Grandma said, "If I know the two of you, you need to get cleaned up."

"Grandma, look at us," Samy said.

"Just as I thought you need to wash your hands and face before you sit down," Grandma said as she looked at the two of us.

Samy and I thought it was hysterical that we had spackle on our noses and laughed a lot as we were washing our hands and face. Then again, there were many things Samy and I found hysterical. The buildings were turning out great and far exceeded our expectations.

Samy explained to Grandma in detail what we had done to our buildings thus far. He recounted our pat-ented gluing procedure, special tool, as well as our mortar job on the buildings. He did so with such passion and thoroughness that sitting there listening to him was a sheer pleasure. The treasure lays not in our buildings, but in the sense of wonder, happiness, and great potential that I see every time I look at my grandson! These were some of the memories, or "snapshots in time" we had created. They would remain in our hearts forever!

*"If you think you can...you will. If you think
you can't... you won't."*

UNKNOWN

CHAPTER 20

If You Think You
CAN...You WILL

Logic will take you from one place to another
however, imagination will take you everywhere.
I shared this with Samy and my grandson's grasp of
this concept astounded me. We had succinctly transformed this idea into "If we can imagine it, we can do
it." This applied to all facets of life where determination
and strength of character were the key components to
achieving one's goals.

Our success had motivated us to move forward in our
journey. We had traveled far, taken "expeditions", done
an incredible amount of research, built our commercial
Victorian buildings, and our plans were on schedule...well

almost! The day arrived when we were going to paint our buildings. Painting, we thought, was going to be the least time consuming and easiest part of completing our buildings. Considering the tiny trim, we thought it would take a few minutes per building. We could not have underestimated the task more!

§

The building trim around the windows was very ornate. The extremely detailed windows necessitated painting with a very thin brush. We soon found out that you needed more than just a thin artist's brush. Masking off those parts of the building that you did not want to get paint on was helpful, but certainly not enough. You really did need the steady hand of an artist and the eye of an eagle. Samy proved that he had both and far exceeded any reasonable expectations for someone his age. We were encouraged by each other and the fact that our turn of the century commercial Victorian structures were turning out so well. Our painting was moving steadily forward but at times seemed torturously slow. Each building had eleven or twelve distinctly separate windows. They also had recessed doorways in front as well as the storefront windows, which were equally ornate.

"Do you think we will be finished this year?" Samy said with a somewhat tortured look on his face.

"I know what you mean, Samy, this is extremely time-consuming and very difficult."

"This reminds me of what Mom always tells me," Samy said thoughtfully.

"Maybe you should share that with me, I could use some encouragement with this painting."

"When something is going to slow or not turning out the way I thought it would, Mom always tells me to have patience and perseverance."

"That is great advice, Samy, especially in situations when you become frustrated with whatever you are doing. Can you imagine it taking four years to paint a ceiling?"

"No I can't, Grandpa that is impossible," Samy answered sure that such a thing was indeed impossible.

"This was no ordinary ceiling. It was the ceiling of the famous Sistine Chapel in Rome. Have you ever heard of it?"

"I don't think so Grandpa. It really took four years to paint the ceiling!" Samy replied still trying to figure out how anyone could take four years to paint a ceiling.

§

I took this opportunity to tell Samy that this was no ordinary ceiling and the painting of it contained works of art much like you would see in a museum. The main area was 131 feet long and forty-three feet wide. Michelangelo was the artist and painter. Originally, he was commissioned to paint only 12 figures, the Apostles. After the work was finished, there were more than 300! His figures showed the Creation, Adam and Eve in the Garden of Eden, and the Great Flood. He started in 1508 and finished in 1512.

"Grandpa, I have heard of Michelangelo and now I think I know why it took so long," Samy responded as the proverbial light bulb went on. I always loved what I called Samy's "light bulb" moments. They were truly something you had to observe first-hand. These moments reminded me of The Fourth of July Fireworks with Samy in the foreground!

I had no reservations whatsoever that Samy did realize that the ceiling of the Sistine Chapel was a work of art. Visualizing something of this nature is difficult for anyone. As always, Samy and I did the "next best thing." We went to the computer to view the ceiling of the Sistine Chapel and read about its history and restoration. I also showed Samy some excellent photographs in a large book I had called The History of Art.

§

Samy and I painted until dinner, and we were both happy to put down our brushes that day. We finished

painting three of the four buildings that needed painting and they looked fantastic! The two of us viewed our
work from all angles around the table that held "our"
masterpieces. We looked for any spots we may have
missed. When we were satisfied that the job was complete, we stepped back and admired our outstanding
work!

"You did a great job, Samy, that wasn't easy," I said
as I thought that painting an entire room in the house
would have been easier. We placed our brushes in the cup
of water on the table and finished for the day.

"You're right, Grandpa, but it wasn't really that hard,
except that you had to concentrate to keep the paint
where you wanted it."

"Tell me something, do you think it was worth it or
should we have bought those inexpensive buildings that
really look like plastic?" I asked him, knowing what his
answer would almost certainly be.

"I think everything we did was worth it, especially the
buildings, our mountain and second level of track," Samy
answered enthusiastically.

"Those 'eagle eyes' of yours were a great help, Is that
why you're able to find the goal on the soccer field?"

"They help, but these do the work," He said pointing
to his legs and feet.

"Do you want to know what muscle does the most
work all of the time?" I asked.

"Which one is that, Grandpa?" He asked, even though I was sure he knew what I was about to say.

"The one located between your ears!" I replied.

§

We turned to go downstairs when Samy asked me if we could look at the ceiling of the Sistine Chapel again. I was impressed with the fact that he indicated a desire to learn more about it and see it on the computer one more time. This desire and curiosity about things past, present, and future should always be encouraged. The images of the Sistine Chapel on the computer gave Samy an idea of the scope, size, and beauty of this work of art. These were biblical stories that Samy was familiar with and came to life on the ceiling of the Sistine Chapel. Samy gave me a short synopsis of the scenes depicted on the ceiling before us.

"While we were painting the trim on our buildings, it did feel as if it was going to take forever," Samy said with the same tortured look I remember seeing during the course of our painting.

"We both felt that way and I am proud that you gave no indication of giving up."

"You know the saying Grandpa, ... "Quitters never win and..."

"Winners never quit," I finished for him.

We went downstairs and our pace was noticeably slower than usual. The painting went well and the buildings looked great, but it had been a very tedious job. I knew that Samy was looking forward to installing the cornices, the film for the windows, and putting the decals on the storefront windows. They even came with cardboard curtains you placed behind the window glass and when the light shined through they looked very authentic. The signs for the storefront windows and the name of each store would give each of the buildings the charm and authenticity we knew was necessary. Samy told me how much he was looking forward to completing the buildings. I marveled at the energy and enthusiasm children have when they become involved in projects such as this. I also knew their potential for learning grew exponentially when they become involved in "doing".

§

Mom and Dad came over that evening and entered the room where our buildings were drying. It was apparent that they were visibly impressed with what they saw. Samy and I think they expected to see buildings that were more like toys. What they saw was authentic replicas of early Victorian commercial buildings.

Mom turned to us and said, "Wow these buildings look tremendous and you haven't even finished them yet!"

"We have to put in the window glass, decals, curtains for the upstairs windows, and then we are going to install the cornices," Samy said excitedly. The torturously slow painting required did not diminish his enthusiasm! It was good to hear the enthusiasm and excitement in Samy's voice and his recall of the facts surrounding The Sistine Chapel was astounding. He relayed the facts he had learned about The Sistine Chapel ceiling to his mother and father better than a tour guide. He explained how it depicted various scenes from the Bible and how it took so long to complete. I could tell by the looks on their faces that Mom and Dad did not expect a history lesson on the Sistine Chapel. I have always believed that under the right circumstances, ordinary projects present opportunities to achieve extraordinary results when children are "involved" in what they do.

Samy gave his Mom and Dad the guided tour explaining how realistic and detailed the buildings were as well as how difficult they were to paint. His father pointed out many details, and elaborated that it is rare to see such trim on modern buildings. It was good to see Samy so engaged and knowledgeable about the historical perspective of the project we had undertaken. Samy's parents were always supportive of whatever he undertook. Whether it is his schoolwork or soccer, they were always there for him. It soon became clear that on this particular day, Samy had exceeded their expectations! I also knew that "exceeding expectations" would become Samy's specialty!

§

Later that evening when the house was very quiet, I went upstairs to shut down my computer. The upstairs hallway connected my office with the room that housed our masterpieces. I could not resist the urge to make the walk down that hallway. This was the same hallway that Samy walked down when he discovered the large walk-in closet and "Old Bob". Once I reached the train room, I marveled at the steady hand and good eye that was evident from the excellent job Samy had done on the buildings he painted. The number and depth of his skills were growing and I wondered which combination of skills he would ultimately choose as a vocation.

Samy had completed painting that day without so much as a whisper of a complaint. He remained positive and showed his patience and perseverance with every brush stroke. The enthusiasm he displayed was indeed contagious and had served us well. We both looked forward to completing our village buildings and moving on to the next phase of our project.

§

I painted the last building that night and left the considerable amount of work we still had for the next time we met. It had been a good day at the S & G Railroad and I looked forward to our next time! Our journey had become much more than the building of the S&G Railroad. It progressed into the creation of memories neither Samy nor I will forget. These "snapshots in time" will live in our hearts forever.

Of course, although I shared Samy's historical perspective, his was viewed through the lens of an eight year old. I was not concerned with "what" Samy would be when he grew up. I knew "who" and "what" kind of person he was already becoming. He is respectful, intelligent, kind, compassionate, and has a strong moral compass.

The time we share together and the bond we create is of paramount importance to me. The lessons learned are important however nothing is as precious to me as the time we spend together. Our journey continues to be a remarkable one and something that will remain in our hearts forever.

"We are what we repeatedly do. Excellence, therefore, is not an act but a habit."

ARISTOTLE

CHAPTER 21

Excellence: Act or Habit?

ailroad stories are part of American History, as well as the history of many countries The stories associated with railroads intertwine with the past and growth of countries throughout the world. Perhaps one of the greatest feelings of satisfaction and enjoyment we get from the history of railroads is the nostalgia associated with it. Railroads take us back in time to an earlier era. They take us back to a time when life was more basic.

Whether or not you are old enough to remember this earlier, simpler time, is made irrelevant by research and imagination. In our complex world, many of us would love to recapture moments from a simpler time. It is an honor to have you accompany us on our journey thus far. Your imagination is all you need to bring with you.

Can you imagine a mode of transportation that was the event and not just a means to an end? Today we rush from place to place making the time it takes to get from one place to another the most important part of the journey. Let us just say for now, that is was not always that way!

§

Determination to build something that was historically accurate was one of our goals. We had completed a considerable amount of research that proved to be increasingly helpful. Our plan had emerged from a desire to build something special we would be proud to display. Our village, although challenging, exhibited this pride and determination as much as it did its turn of the century Victorian architecture. We underestimated the time it would take to complete our buildings, but Samy and I agreed that this only made it even more special! The extremely detailed cornices were next on our list. We had learned from experience that "extremely detailed" translated into "difficult to paint." Samy and I considered every difficult task a challenge and every problem an opportunity. We were determined to finish painting the trim on our buildings, install the window glass, curtains and cornices today. When Samy arrived, I had everything we needed ready to go.

"Grandpa, do you think we will finish the buildings today?" Samy said with a very determined tone in his voice that made his question more of a statement.

"I think that will depend on how difficult cutting and installing the window glass will be, but it shouldn't be as tedious as the gluing and painting was."

"You can say that again, Grandpa!"

"O.K., I think that will depend on how difficult cutting and..."

"Oh Grandpa..."

Just once I would like to slip one of these comments by Samy without him noticing. I was beginning to doubt whether that would ever happen. At least I knew that Samy was listening!

We measured the windows on the inside carefully, and thankfully they all were the same size. We then measured the storefront windows and they too were very close in size. After we measured and wrote everything down, we decided to tape them in place one building at a time. Our first building was completely finished in less than 30 minutes and the remaining three took us an additional hour. Samy was taping in the last of the windows and I was cutting out the thin cardboard curtains. We put the curtains in place and it was time for us to step back and admire and evaluate what we had done!

§

All that was left of what proved to be one of the most challenging parts of our journey together were the cornices and the decals for the storefront windows. The decals for the windows would add to the Victorian charm of our buildings. The cornices may have been extremely difficult to paint, but exemplified the architecture and extreme detail that was characteristic of the era. They were the most dramatic feature that each of our buildings possessed. Combined with all of the ornate trim, they definitely made our buildings very special.

"Let's start with the drug store first and put the name of the store on first and then the advertisements for the windows," Samy said with his usual enthusiasm for every project he takes on.

"That sounds like a good plan to me."

Samy placed the name of the drug store in the three transoms of the storefront

"Look, Grandpa they fit perfectly!" Samy said excitedly as he carefully pushed each in place. He then placed the "Prescriptions filled while you wait" and the "10% off cosmetics" signs in the drug store windows.

"Samy, that looks so real. I feel like it's the turn of the century and we are standing in front of a real drug store."

The next building we decided to put the final additions on was the most ornate. This was the local restaurant called "Vinny's Grill." Samy put the name on it and I put the "Daily Lunch Specials" sign in the window.

The bakery name, which Samy had already installed, was "Pedicini's Bakery." We then put in the sign that said "Fresh Baked Daily" over the door and the "Bagels", "Donuts" and "Wedding Cake" signs in the front windows as well!

Our post office had a rectangular cornice across the top with a space to which we attached the words "United States Post Office".

The buildings were complete at last! We congratulated one another once again and were extremely pleased with the results of our effort.

"Grandpa, you did a great job on these buildings, a really great job!"

"You mean 'we' did a great job."

The buildings were exact replicas of the type of commercial Victorian architecture that had spread across America with the growth of the railroads. We sat down together and admired our work. Samy commented on how the stores looked and felt like the hardware store in the center of our town that opened in 1900. We were fortunate to have the opportunity to see and experience one of these stores ourselves, just as it was when it opened in 1900!

§

"Did they have electricity in the buildings built in the late 1800s and early 1900s?" Samy asked.

"The invention of the first practical light bulb became a reality in 1879. Few people had electricity to power a light bulb. It was in the 1880s that the first power grid came on line to light a few city blocks in New York City. The short answer to your question is they did not have electricity in the hardware store when it was first built."

"When was the first steam engine invented?" Samy asked enthusiastically.

"Now that is a difficult question to answer because I am pretty sure you mean the first railroad engine, which was the result of the efforts and work of many men."

We decided to look it up and we found that in 1813, George Stephenson became aware that William Hedley and Timothy Hackworth were designing a locomotive for the Wylam coal mine in England. At the age of twenty, George Stephenson began the construction of his first locomotive. It should be noted that at this time in history, every part of the engine had to be made by hand, and hammered into shape just like a horseshoe. John Thorswall, a coal mine blacksmith, was George Stephenson's main assistant.

After ten months' labor, George Stephenson's locomotive "Blucher" was completed and tested on the Collingwood Railway on July 25, 1814. The track was an uphill trek of four hundred and fifty feet. George Stephenson's engine hauled eight loaded coal wagons weighing thirty tons, at about four miles an hour. This was the first steam engine powered locomotive to run on a railroad and it was the most successful working steam engine that had ever been constructed up to this period. This encouraged the inventor to make further experiments. In all, Stephenson built sixteen different engines.

George Stephenson built the world's first public railways. The Stockton and Darlington railway was built in 1825 and the Liverpool-Manchester railway in 1830. Stephenson was the chief engineer for several of the railways built during this time.

"That was in England, when did the railroad cross the United States?" Samy asked.

"There were early railroad lines in the United States before the Civil War in 1860. If you are asking when the first railroad actually crossed the entire United States that did not happen until 1870," I said very happy to answer Samy's question. It was gratifying to see such an interest in history on Samy's part.

In 1870, the tracks met in Promontory Point, Utah with much celebration. America now had a truly transcontinental railroad. The companies that built these railroads did so at great cost. The laborers that laid the track, that would eventually connect East and West, suffered greatly and many lives were lost in the process.

"I think you can see that the rail lines that existed in the early 1900's were a result of the cumulative efforts of many men dating back over 100 years! This was true of many of the famous inventions of the late 19th and early 20th century."

"So our town, the one we built on our layout, was not just a railroad town." Samy stated with somewhat of a question mark in his voice.

"That is very perceptive, Samy, it was established before and grew in part because the railroads now made it possible for people to come to our area, farm the land and ship their crops to market by rail."

"Did most people drive cars in our area in 1900 when our town was established? When was the airplane invented?" He asked, exhibiting a genuine curiosity about the development of these inventions and the impact they made on people's lives.

"Wilbur and Orville Wright made their first successful flight in 1903, but I doubt if you would fly with them."

"It wasn't really for passengers?" he asked.

"Not yet, but In 1925 however, the Ford Motor Company bought out the Stout Aircraft Company and began construction of the all-metal Ford Trimotor, which became the first successful American airliner. With a 12-passenger capacity, the Trimotor made passenger service potentially profitable. Air service was seen as a supplement to rail service in the American transportation network."

"What about cars, Grandpa, did a lot of people drive cars?"

"The simple answer is not yet, because the first motorized assembly lines were not in place until 1913 and very few people could afford to own one. This changed in the 1920's and 30's."

"It's hard to imagine living without lights, cars, and everything we have that runs on electricity." These were words spoken in a manner that indicated that Samy could live without them if he had to.

"What would you do if the electricity was shut off and when you walked into a room you couldn't just flip a switch to turn on the lights? What about the refrigerator, computer, and television?" It was easy to see the "wheels turning" as Samy was thinking about his response.

"I guess if the lights went out we could light candles, but keeping food cold would be a problem. Television, anyone should be able to live without, but I would like to find a way to power a computer." Samy paused for a moment and then said, "We would find another way to make electricity so everything would work again." Samy often demonstrates his ability to hypothesize when presented with such problems.

"Would you say life was simpler without all the 'stuff' we accumulate, and in the days when you did not have something you didn't miss it? Have we come to depend on these things too much without giving any thought to the fact that there was a day when they did not exist?"

Samy thought for a minute before answering and said, "We do have too much 'stuff' and there are many things we could do without. There are many things that help us that we should keep."

"I would have to agree, most of our life-saving equipment would not exist if we did not have the inventions you refer to, and build on them."

"I thought of a way to keep food cool...actually a couple of ways," he said proudly.

"How could we do that, Samy?" I asked looking forward to Samy's answer.

"If it's winter we could keep them outside and in the summer we could insulate a big box and put it in the ground where it usually stays cool."

This was exactly the kind of response Samy so often exhibited. His critical thinking skills seemed to "kick in" at just the right time, and I loved being there to see him in action.

"Good thinking, Samy that is a great idea!"

"Thanks, Grandpa" he said very proud of himself.

"Someday you may be part of the history books for inventing the 'Gumazegong'!"

"Oh Grandpa...!"

§

Although the railroads remained America's most important transportation system for the first few decades of the twentieth century, their glory days were over. The railroads did not "own" the twentieth century in the same way they had "owned" the late nineteenth century. Travel by car, tour bus, and soon, by plane, started the decline of passenger travel. The railroad industry faced competition from the emerging economical trucking industry, which promised to take up a large share of the freight business.

There is no denying that this era in our history played an important role in our growth as a nation. Stories and legends from turn of the century America are fascinating. When we recreate something from a particular era, it ignites an interest in history. Perhaps this is why model railroading is so cool. It is the fusion of working with actual scale models, historical perspective and working with someone, you love.

Model Railroading is a multi-faceted hobby. There are many aspects to it that simply cannot be found anywhere. We embraced all of them and proceeded with our journey. The interest, the history and the multi-generational aspect of our journey transformed the "hobby" into a "journey" for us. The skills used and developed I truly believe are secondary to the memories and the satisfaction of a job well done. Contrary to what many people may think, you do not need to be a carpenter or an electrician to become involved with this tremendous hobby. When was the last time you played a video game and said this one will be close to my heart forever? When you said, "I will always remember when I watched that television show?" I thought so.

Samy and I will always remember what we have learned in the course of our journey. More importantly, we will always remember the experience of taking the journey together! These are the "snapshots in time" we will cherish forever.

> *"Without continual growth and progress, such words as improvement, achievement, and success have no meaning."*
>
> BENJAMIN FRANKLIN

CHAPTER 22

The Trolley and a Surprise

"Grandpa, we really should lay the tracks for the trolley in front of our village area before we do anything else. We could use the tracks that came with 'Old Bob' because they will look more like trolley tracks," Samy said as he surveyed the area in front of our village.

"That is a great idea, Samy. Did you know that there was a trolley in front of the hardware store in the center of our town?"

He hesitated a moment, clearly thinking about something, then said, "I wish there was a trolley there now, it would be so cool to ride past all the turn of the century buildings in town on a trolley." Samy has a genuine appreciation for the "essence" of history as well as for the facts surrounding the period we were discussing. The differences between our modern lifestyle in the twenty-first century and the early twentieth century are certainly not lost on him.

We assembled the small oval of track in front of our buildings and wired them to our trolley's transformer. He peered out from behind the buildings on the opposite side of our layout, and said, "Grandpa, all we need now is the trolley!"

"Do you remember where we put it Samy?" The trolley we purchased quite some time ago was stored in our former hallway linen closet, which had now become the S & G Railroad supply closet. There was no doubt that he would remember where we had put it for safekeeping. His capacity to remember even the smallest details is extraordinary!

"It's on the top shelf in our closet in the original box it came in," Samy replied without hesitation, remembering where we had put it over a year ago.

We placed the trolley on the tracks and made sure all of the connections were tight on both the track and transformer. Samy took control of the transformer that powered our trolley, and slowly raised the lever that controlled the speed of the trolley. The lights inside the trolley went on, and it began to make its way around our village, just as it did in the early 1900s!

"Grandpa, that looks so cool!" He immediately experimented with various speeds to make sure our trolley passed all of our safety standards. The trolley passed with "flying colors" and we both agreed it made a great addition to our village and to the overall authenticity and realism of our layout.

"Samy, do you remember the track we saw online when we were researching buildings for our village? It was thin and was made to look exactly like part of the road we will be putting in front of our village."

"The rails were built in the track instead of being raised and the rest was black just like a road would be and it would be perfect for our trolley," Samy replied.

Why should I be surprised that he would recall the track we had seen? The manufacturer of the track could not have given a better description. This was part of the description of the track displayed on the manufacturer's website. Samy's description included the benefit it afforded to anyone using a trolley!

"Let's go to our online library and look it up, Samy, I bookmarked the sight just in case we wanted to return to it."

The computer had served us well in our research of the period in history in which we were interested. It had also become our home library. We could not locate the "bookmark" so we typed in a search on the computer and it was not long before we were looking at the track we wanted.

The track had to be the right gauge for our trolley and had to pass the "authenticity test" for use in our village. The rails came built in the "street" which made it perfect for our trolley, and extremely authentic.

"We should keep the old track on for now and when we finish our village we should order the new track," Samy suggested.

"That sounds like a great plan, and it will give us time to finish some of the scenery we talked about."

§

Samy did not know at that time that I had plans to extend our layout by adding a section at one end. The new section would be approximately three and one half feet wide by four feet long. It would make our table "L" shaped and give us the ability to make a huge oval that connected with the upper section of our existing track. A switch placed on both sides of the oval would allow the train on the upper section of track to cross over the lower section at two places. I knew this rather aggressive plan necessitated the construction of a bridge across the entire layout. This bridge would be almost six feet long and approximately six inches wide.

The next time Samy walked into the room a few days later, he spotted the addition, and the look on his face displayed a mixture of disbelief, excitement, and pure joy!

"Grandpa, thank you so much, now we have a place for a rail yard to park the trains on the lower part of the addition you built."

The wood that would serve as the road or "surface" of the bridge was cut, and fitted to size. This included the curves at each end that made it almost parallel to the existing track. The only thing that remained was to construct the support pillars under the roadbed of the bridge itself. Samy and I had decided to have our bridge remain as authentic as possible. The roadbed was in place held up by pieces of two inch by four-inch pieces of lumber. Screws from underneath our layout would hold the "pillars" in place.

"Does the Rockville Bridge sound familiar to you?" I asked Samy.

"I think we saw it when we were on the computer, but I'm not sure." Samy answered.

"You're right, you did see it, and it's the world's longest stone arch bridge. It crosses over the Susquehanna River in Pennsylvania. In 1902 The Rockville Bridge made its debut and measured 3,820 feet long. It is made almost entirely out of stone, and is one of the world's oldest and most famous bridges of its kind." I added.

"I know exactly the one you are talking about Grandpa. It has a lot of arches and is made of stone. We could have the lower track pass through an arch and maybe even a stream or a river," Samy said as if the proverbial light bulb had gone off.

"That's the one we saw that is still in use today over 100 years later. You are right, we can finally have everything you wanted on our layout including two places where the trains will pass over or under one another."

"Thank you Grandpa, that is going to be the longest bridge ever on a train layout," he said wide-eyed and with a grin from ear to ear!

"What material do you think we should use for the sides of the bridge?" We had worked with a variety of different materials, and I truly could not wait to hear what his answer would be. We were now about to create a bridge made almost entirely of stone!

"I think we should do exactly what you did to make the stone walls underneath the upper section of track. We should use thick cardboard, cut out the arches, and wrap them with plaster cloth," Samy said without the least bit of hesitation.

"A superb idea, you may become a world-famous architect someday, only then you will be working with materials a little bit stronger than plaster cloth and cardboard."

Samy was busy examining the bridge span to see how tall and wide we needed to make the arches, especially the ones at the ends of the bridge where it would go over track. We used our tallest train car, which happened to be a car carrier to determine the height our arches needed to be. Several derailments later, and a great deal of laughing, we knew the exact height it must be. In the interest of safety as well as preparing for any oversized loads, we decided to add an inch to the height of our original measurement.

"Grandpa, I think that about does it for the measurements of the bridge and the arches." Samy was now convinced we had considered every possible scenario, and our measurements allowed for the height of any future loads.

"I think you're right, all we have to do is screw our supports in place, and we will be ready to make the arches that really give this bridge its strength, not to mention its character."

We measured the eight supports and put them in place. Samy outlined each with a pencil and we took turns drilling a hole in the center of each outline through the table. When we finished, Samy replaced the supports using the outline as a guide, held them tightly in place, and I put a two and a half inch screw in to each from underneath the layout.

I was in the process of getting out from under the layout when Samy said, "These are really strong," as he tried to move each one like a safety engineer checking for structural defects.

"Are they strong like rocks?" I asked.

"No they are strong like Rockville!" He answered laughing and showing his dimples.

"Together we have followed and crossed over the rocks in the stream, gathered rocks for the base of our mountain, positioned rocks around the old mine we created, filled our stream bed with rocks, built a rock wall next to our roadbed, sat on the huge rock wall together on our expedition, and now we are building the Rockville Bridge!"

"You forgot the boulders behind the rock wall on our first expedition and 'Boulder Point back in the 1950s," Samy added.

I could not be happier that Samy had remembered and I answered with "I guess it's been a 'rocky journey' so far but one I am enjoying immensely."

Both Samy and I began to laugh, partially because we had worked so hard that day, but mostly because we were enjoying ourselves! By the end of the day, we had accomplished quite a lot of work. Our village, school, church, and log cabin were all in place. The bridge was now structurally sound and able to hold the track. The stonework and arches would follow shortly. Samy and I were now looking forward to the grand opening of our bridge. The trolley had found a home and added the authenticity and charm we wanted for our layout.

§

"Why don't towns have trolleys anymore, when they seem like such a good idea?" Samy asked, somewhat perplexed by the idea that people would stop using something that was a perfectly good idea.

"Do you remember the invention that people accepted so quickly when it became affordable? This invention was partly responsible for the decline of the trolley."

"You mean the car was the reason we don't see trolleys anymore?" Samy said with a definite tone of disbelief in his voice.

"The automobile and the bus were responsible for a steady decline in ridership beginning in the 1920's. That does not mean that people stopped using them completely. They were fascinated with the automobile and the freedom and speed it gave them to go almost anywhere. Buses did the same thing as trolleys and were faster." I added.

"The companies that built the trolley cars and laid the track in the streets knew people were not going to ride on them as much, so they stopped building them," Samy said thoughtfully.

"I would say your analysis is very accurate, and sometimes when we look back at things like the trolley it can be sad. We must look ahead and improve upon them for the future."

§

Samy was growing physically, emotionally, intellectually and spiritually. He has never stopped leaving his footprints on my heart and soul. When we are together, his sense of wonder and humor combine with an intellectual curiosity that amazes me in ways one can only imagine.

"Things do not change; we change."

HENRY DAVID THOREAU

CHAPTER 23

Change and Imagination

𝕰very child has capabilities that are often far beyond the traditionally academic. Many people did fairly well in school due to their high academic ability. High academic ability is not a guarantee that their creative thinking and problem-solving skills developed accordingly. Parents and Grandparents can do many things to support what goes on in the classroom.

Creativity demands that we involve our young people and encourage imaginative thinking and behavior. Creativity and imagination can be powerful partners when they are purposeful. I encouraged Samy to always ask questions, see things in his "mind's eye", and always imagine the possibilities. We strived hard to recreate our village, track, and mountains to be as historically accurate as possible. The creativity and imagination Samy exhibited was in "how" to make this possible.

Our journey into the past was based not only on the facts we knew, but also in our ability to imagine being there. Our journey into the future necessitated being able to see things in our mind's eye and say this could be possible. In any event, our journey together had become one filled with the unknown and Samy and I looked forward to not knowing what would come next!

Our "master plan" took a new direction at every stage of our journey. The one thing that remained constant was that we were never quite sure of what lay around the bend. The journey we were on became an adventure into the unknown. Like the railroad, it had evolved into something much bigger than we had planned and we were happy that the ever-changing nature of our project only added to the excitement and challenges it presented.

§

How would we have reacted if someone told us we were going to build a thirty inch high mountain range with two tunnels through it, a second level of track, an authentic replica of a turn of the century town, and a bridge that is over 65 inches long? We would probably have told them that it would take the combined resources of two model railroading clubs to do something on this scale and degree of authenticity! Together, we did build all of that and more! We had the drive and enthusiasm for what we were doing and we enjoyed every minute of it.

The sides of the Rockville Bridge were challenging. The arches had to be accurately spaced and of equal size with the exception of where the bridge crossed the track on each end. We cut out a long rectangular piece of cardboard for each side of the bridge. It was slightly larger than six inches high by sixty-eight inches long! Now we needed a "pattern" for each arch that we could trace and cut out to maintain uniformity. Several experimental cuts later, we had the pattern for our arches that were the proper size and allowed for future growth!

We temporarily installed the sides of our bridge to sketch the arches on each end. Samy had his architect/engineer's hat on that day. He looked up from the bridge he was sitting next to and said quite emphatically "Grandpa, let's make another stencil for the arch, and you can do one side and I'll trace the other."

Samy was waiting for a response that did not come quickly. Thoughts of how his organizational skills were developing took precedence over our project for a moment. This soon-to-be eight-year-old now initiated action, rather than just wait for instructions to follow.

"Grandpa, what do you think?" Samy said impatiently waiting for an answer.

"I think your idea is a good one and it will certainly speed things up if we each take one side."

We brought the sides to the floor and began tracing the arches out carefully making sure they would line up correctly on each side. It was not long before we reached the cutting stage of our bridge project and I suggested that I would do the cutting with a very sharp hobby knife.

"Grandpa, can I try if I promise to be careful?" Samy said after a few of the arches were cut out.

"Sure Samy, just remember to hold the knife with the point facing down like this."

"I'll be careful, Grandpa."

"Just remember it's you not the project that I worry about. We can always do something over."

Samy took over and started cutting like a professional "arch cutter." His game face was on, and he was concentrating on every millimeter of each arch. His laser vision and excellent eye-hand coordination enabled him to make almost perfect cuts.

"These are outstanding cuts you made, I am really impressed! You're not getting older, you're getting better!" I said with a genuinely sincere tone in my voice.

"Thanks Grandpa, the first one was a little bit hard but after that the others weren't so bad."

We put the sides with the arches cut out, against both sides of the bridge, and when we were satisfied that everything lined up perfectly, we brought them to our plaster table.

"Do you remember when we built the mountain and covered it with plaster cloth, Grandpa?" Samy said enthusiastically.

"How can I forget? That was more like a sculpture, but this should be pretty straightforward and the plaster will take on the appearance of stone or brick."

Samy was an "old pro" at this by now and he proceeded to cut the plaster cloth into strips. Each of his strips was about four inches wide and I asked him how he arrived at the size of the strips.

"I remember the mountain and it didn't make any difference how big the strips were because the mountain was so big. On the bridge we want it flat and not squished."

"Good thinking Samy, they could have used you when they built the Rockville Bridge."

"I would be pretty old by now, Grandpa." Samy laughed, once again displaying a sense of humor beyond his years.

§

"Did you know that there were two other bridges built over the Susquehanna River on the exact same spot?"

"Really Grandpa," Samy answered with a puzzled look on his face.

"The first was a wooden bridge completed in 1849 that did not have much traffic and what little traffic it did have, was lighter. It fell apart and they built a new iron bridge in 1877, when train traffic increased. The iron bridge did not do well due to the increased traffic and storms. It was decided that the only material that would withstand the increased traffic, heavy loads, and weather was stone."

"Our bridge will last longer than all of them, Grandpa." Samy replied as if he somehow knew that our bridge would indeed last forever. It will live on in our hearts and minds along with the special memories associated with our journey together.

We finished our "stonework" on the bridge that day and the result was spectacular. Samy placed the car carrier on the track, and we were ready for our final safety check. The car rolled under it with room to spare. After we cleaned up, we could not break with tradition, which dictated that now was the time to step back, congratulate each other, and simply admire our creation!

"We are really getting there, Samy. Everything we have done so far has come out great and we built everything ourselves."

"I really think the stores we built from the kits look just like the real thing," Samy stated emphatically.

"The log cabin, school, and church look great also."

"There is one thing we built that stands out when you look at our layout and we built it all," Samy said proudly.

We turned toward one another with big smiles on our faces and said at the same time "The Mountain". This was our crowning achievement, especially with the addition of the tunnels and the trees we had planted on it. The waterfall, which we made provision for on the mountain would be "Icing on the cake". Ironically, the mountain we built was not something we had seen or came in a kit. We did not send away for mountain building books or scenery catalogues. The mountain was truly our own creation with most of the credit going to Samy for its shape, size, and ridges. This was a fact Samy and I had discussed many times. It also was an extension of "If you think you Can ... you Will, If you think you Can't ... you Won't."

"Some of the most creative things we did were a result of imagining them and then going ahead and building!"

"You are right Grandpa, the mountain was like that, the tunnels, and the abandoned mine!"

We also had built a replica of an old abandoned gold or silver mine at the edge of our mountain range with timbers we distressed to appear old. Samy had suggested the mine when we were talking about features you might find in a region such as our mountain range.

Our railroad yard consisted of two semi-circular track areas switched from our main line. Switches allowed us, at the precise moment, to turn off the track power in the train yard from our control panel. We switched the power on in the train yard when we wanted to bring a particular train back to the main track.

§

Time had flown by so quickly and we both agreed that it seemed like only yesterday that we made our amazing archaeological discovery in our highly classified room! I assured my grandson that creating memories such as these were important and finding "Old Bob" served as a catalyst for our project.

"Did you ever think we were going to have such a big layout with so many different things on it?" Samy asked as if a plan was in place he did not know about.

"Samy, these things, especially when we are involved, take on a life of their own and continue to grow. They are also part of a much longer journey. Are you happy with the way it is turning out and with what you have learned?"

"I'm more than happy Grandpa, when we first started all we had was 'Old Bob,' and three feet of old track!" Samy replied with his characteristic enthusiasm.

"Shh, not so loud, 'Old Bob' might hear you and take it the wrong way and I know you wouldn't want to hurt his feelings."

"Old Bob deserves all the credit for our project and for giving us our inspiration!" Samy said this in the same manner you would if you were recognizing a person for outstanding achievement.

"I seem to remember a certain little boy inspiring me to begin a journey, the nature of which no one could have foreseen. Do you know who that little boy is?"

"That was me, but you did help a little bit," Samy said with a huge smile that seemed to reach from ear to ear. He barely finished his sentence when he broke out in laughter.

"You asked for it now," I said as I immediately attacked my grandson and began to tickle him. "You forgot, I know where all your 'tickle spots' are!"

Samy's laughter was music to my ears and something I cherished. The tickling and laughter lasted for quite some time. Opportunities like this one make our most cherished memories possible. The "snapshots in time" we create will last forever!

"*Blessed are those that can give cheerfully without remembering and receive without forgetting.*"

UNKNOWN

CHAPTER 24

𝕿𝖍𝖆𝖓𝖐𝖘𝖌𝖎𝖛𝖎𝖓𝖌... "𝕻𝖎𝖈𝖐𝖎𝖓𝖌 𝖀𝖕 𝕾𝖙𝖊𝖆𝖒"

Thanksgiving Day means many things to many people. Throughout the years, it has always been distinctive because of its association with family. Many families separated by geography or other factors make a special effort to get together on Thanksgiving Day. As a young boy, I remember getting into the car as a family and driving to our grandparent's home where our aunts, uncles, and cousins would gather to give thanks to our Creator for all the blessings He had bestowed on us that year. Later on in life, it took on an even greater significance. Thanksgiving was the only holiday that people of all faiths celebrated together.

This year we would be celebrating Thanksgiving at Samy's other grandparent's home. They lived approximately 35 minutes away and had moved here from the very same northern state where Grandma and Grandpa grew up and where Samy's mom and dad were raised. Fortunately, Samy would have the opportunity to spend special holidays like this with his parents, grandparents, aunts, uncles, and cousins.

It had become a tradition, before eating all the scrumptious food, that so many hands had prepared, for each person to thank God for that which they were most thankful. When it was my turn I always mentioned the blessing called "Samy" which was bestowed upon me. When specifically mentioned by name Samy would simply smile without the least hint of any embarrassment that many children might exhibit. This day provided Samy with an opportunity to play with and see all his cousins.

§

Good times like this always seem to pass much too quickly. Christmas was just around the corner and like most seven year olds Samy was preparing his list for Santa. We viewed many different accessories and trains during our online research and Samy had consistently asked about a Santa Fe engine and tender. The engine was a 2-8-4 replica of one of the most powerful steam engines ever built.

This engine, with its silver front where the chimney, bell, and light were housed, was as attractive as it was powerful. The roof over the rear of the engine where the engineer sat was red. The tender also had this splash of red on it and the words "Santa Fe" on the side.

"Grandpa, this is just about the coolest steam engine I've ever seen and maybe I should put this on my list for Santa this year."

"Cooler than the Milwaukee," I asked?

"Not cooler than the Milwaukee, but the best steam engine I've seen." Samy replied enthusiastically.

Although we had seen this engine many times before, Samy became particularly excited because it seemed quite logical that this steam engine and tender should be included on his list for Santa this year. "Why don't we look up the history of this particular engine," I said, leading Samy to make a discovery on his own.

We searched for and found that it was one of several 2-8-4 steam engines built for various railroad companies across the United States. A western company purchased this engine for their rail lines near New Mexico. "Do you think that the Santa Fe would be appropriate for our rail line, located in the eastern part of the country," I asked.

"Probably not, but I still like this engine and it's the best one I've seen," Samy said thoughtfully.

"Even though we have tried to be authentic in every detail of our layout, it would still be alright if we put this engine on our railway," I replied.

"Isn't the Rockville Bridge we built located in Pennsylvania Grandpa?" Samy asked. We were on eBay at the time admiring the Santa Fe engine and tender and I was sure he was definitely leading me somewhere and it could only be to one place.

"Yes it is, Samy," I answered with somewhat of a question mark in my voice.

Samy became very animated and said very enthusiastically, "Why don't we type in Pennsylvania railroad steam engines in the search?"

I smiled and said, "Because I can't spell Pennsylvania?"

"Oh G r a n d p a!..."

We typed in the search for "Pennsylvania Steam Engines" and we received thirteen pages of results. When we were on the ninth page of both old and new engines we decided that there was a possibility that the engine we were searching for was never made. We reached the last page of the search results, and still no Pennsylvania steam engine.

"What do you think we should do next?" At this point Samy looked disappointed but determined.

"Why don't we try that hobby shop where you bought the track and transformer," Samy said thoughtfully.

"Good thinking, Samy it's worth a try," I said while typing in the name of the hobby shop. We found the hobby store we were looking for but they did not offer the engine we wanted and we were running out of options.

Samy suggested that we change our strategy and revised our search to "Berkshire Steam Engines." Our new search yielded only four pages of results. We carefully reviewed each page and on the last page, we finally struck gold! There it was in all its glory "Pennsylvania Steam Locomotive #2356." It was an exact duplicate of the Santa Fe that Samy liked so much only with the addition of train and rail sounds!

"Grandpa, that's the one, it's the exact same one except it has 'Pennsylvania Railroad' written on the side and the other engine had 'Santa Fe' on it," Samy shouted enthusiastically.

We clicked on the picture and brought up a larger picture with a more detailed description. The description included the fact that we were indeed looking at the fast, powerful locomotive that raced through the rugged Allegheny Mountains and crossed over the three rivers including the Susquehanna River by way of the Rockville Bridge.

"Grandpa, do they mean the same Rockville Bridge that we built for our layout?" By now, Samy was more than excited and from where I sat, that was a very good thing.

At this point, it was difficult to tell who was more excited! This engine would make a great addition to the

S&G Railroad. It was authentic, detailed, geographically correct, and the timing could not have been better!

"It gets even better, Samy, take a good look at the specifications on this one," I said enthusiastically.

"It says that it has the sound of steam chuffing, steam whistle, bell, squealing breaks, and operator controlled multi-part crew dialogue. This is one really cool engine and it even has a headlight that works!"

Samy was excited about what we had found and what made it even better was the fact that it fit in with the "authenticity protocols" we had established. The engine was loaded with a host of features that would make any youngster excited beyond measure. I was getting more excited as I listened to the description Samy was reading.

"Samy, check this out. It has an operating coupler on the rear of the tender, a maintenance-free motor, momentum flywheel, traction tires, engineer and fireman figures, and puffing smoke."

"What is a momentum flywheel?" Samy said somewhat puzzled by its name.

"It stores some of the energy that is created by the motor of the train and basically makes it perform smoother. We will have to look it up for more details."

"I see the little figures inside the engine and they do make it look more realistic just like our village," Samy commented with a certain presence and authority that only comes with experience.

"Does it meet all of the criteria for our layout and pass all of the tests for authenticity and realism?" I asked knowing that the answer I would get would be both truthful and accurate.

"It sure does Grandpa, it's extremely detailed, really powerful, and has so many features!"

"Samy, correct me if I'm wrong, but I am getting the impression that you like this engine!" We clearly were both excited and I could see Samy was on cloud nine.

"Grandpa this engine is definitely going on my list for Santa. This has got to be the world's greatest engine!"

§

We must have stared at the pictures on the screen before us for an hour that day marveling at the metal construction and fine details. It was not difficult to become caught up in the moment. We were finding new details on the engine and tender the longer we scrutinized the pictures before us. The only question was which one of us was more excited.

The timing could not have been better. Christmas was only three weeks away and Samy's eighth birthday was not long after that. Soon, we would be visiting the Botanical Gardens and Santa Claus. It seemed like yesterday that we had visited with Santa at these beautiful gardens. Time does have a way of passing by to quickly which is why it is up to each of us to make sure we make productive use of it. The time spent with Samy may sometimes be productive, but is always precious. We leave behind birdhouses, bird condos, model planes, tall ships, and stories about medieval castles, bed racing, and many more activities.

What is most important is the irreplaceable time we spend doing them together. We may be in the process of completing an excellent train layout, but the innumerable memories we create in doing so, and the journey we are on together are priceless!

"Unless we make Christmas an occasion to share our blessings, all the snow in Alaska won't make it 'white'."

BING CROSBY

CHAPTER 25

𝕾𝖍𝖆𝖗𝖊𝖉 𝕭𝖑𝖊𝖘𝖘𝖎𝖓𝖌𝖘

The Christmas Season is rich with many precious memories. The celebration of Hanukkah fell more closely to December 25th than any time in recent memory this year. This made the celebration of both holidays even more special. What if we could in some way preserve the feeling one gets at this magical time of year when someone wishes you a "Merry Christmas" or a "Happy Hanukah?" The same sentiments expressed during the weeks leading up to this special time of year should last throughout the year.

Samy and I were excited that our next "planned" expedition was to visit Santa at the Botanical Gardens to keep the family tradition alive. The magic and excitement

when we talked about our upcoming visit showed themselves in the eyes of my very special partner. Samy knew
the true meaning of Christmas and that giving was more
important than receiving. He also knew that filling that
shoebox with toys for boys and girls less fortunate than
he exemplified the true meaning of Christmas. He did so
willingly and was perhaps one of the most "cheerful giv-
ers" I have ever seen.

§

We were discussing our upcoming trip to visit with
Santa when he turned and asked thoughtfully, "Did people celebrate Christmas like we do during the building of
the railroads?" His question was not surprising since he
had asked me similar questions during the course of our
"journey" together.

"The true meaning of Christmas has not changed.
What you have to keep in mind is that so many different people came to America during the 1700s and 1800s
and brought with them different ways they celebrated
Christmas in the countries they came from."

"Did they put Christmas trees in their houses the way
we do now?" Samy asked pinpointing one of the most
popular and loved Christmas traditions.

"The Christmas tree was originally a German tradition
seen only in the homes of German-Americans. Americans

decided to adopt this tradition as their own and during the 1850s town squares began to put up Christmas trees." Samy was beginning to ask more insightful questions as time progressed.

"Our hardware store that was started in 1900 probably sold Christmas trees."

"We would have to do a little research on that to be sure but by 1900 it was estimated that one American in five had a Christmas tree. Even Jewish children at the turn of the century wanted a Christmas tree, so you see it certainly was not a religious symbol."

"Did people give presents to one another the way we do now, Grandpa?"

"If you go further back in time it was the custom of many to give gifts they created themselves. Can you imagine how many gifts you would receive if that were true today?"

"Probably not as many, but we still could have made our projects like our birdhouses, mountains, and even the houses we made." Samy said with a great deal of pride and satisfaction.

"You are absolutely right Samy, but as time went on Christmas became more commercial and people began to 'buy' more presents. It is important that we remember the true meaning of all of our holidays."

"Making a present for someone is a good idea. Anyone can buy a present but when you make something for someone they know you spent your time doing it for them." Samy's comment made it clear to me that he did indeed grasp the concept of the uniqueness of this type of gift giving and left me speechless.

§

The air was crisp and cold that winter evening. Even the smell in the air that night told me it was going to snow. There had always been something special about a white Christmas. Those of us who grew up in an area of the country where this was common secretly wished for it. Bing Crosby sang about it, Charles Dickens wrote about it, and Jimmy Stewart starred in it. Santa lives at the North Pole where there is certainly no shortage of it!

Grandma and Grandpa picked up Mom, Dad, and Samy and we were off to visit Santa at the Botanical Gardens just a forty-mile sleigh ride from our home. Samy had already emailed his list to Santa. He realized that there was nothing better than delivering it in person. This was our third Christmas visit to Santa at one of the most beautiful places one could imagine. Santa was royalty this night and his subjects were coming to visit. The Botanical Gardens were a fitting backdrop for such an important occasion.

Our family outing was more than a trip to the mall to see Santa. It had become more of a family tradition that we hoped would last a very long time. Samy has grown in so many ways, and his eagerness to visit with Santa grew with him. There was no doubt about what was on the top of Samy's list this year and it had the number 2356 printed on it!

We were very close to the entrance of the dazzling 400-acre estate that was home to the gardens. If you looked carefully, you could see the glow from the expertly illuminated trees that lined the entrance. Listen closely, and you may even hear sleigh bells!

We drove through the entrance and tens of thousands of twinkling Christmas lights that lined the long winding road greeted us on our way to the main building. There were decorations and lights as far as the eye could see. Even though we had been there before the grounds were no less spectacular. The main entrance was decorated with evergreens and trees made entirely out of orchids. There were enormous bows and ribbons everywhere. This beautiful building became a magical palace during this very special time of year. Samy commented on the orchids and the enormous bows and how much work it must be to make this transformation possible.

"Grandpa, Did they change anything or add more since last year?" Samy asked inquisitively.

"If you came here and spent five days each year, you probably would not see everything, so it might seem like they did."

Samy agreed that there was an awful lot to see and that he wanted to find out if Santa was in the same place. We also wanted to locate the train set that was set up in one of the rooms last year. The train exhibit was in the same place we discovered it the year before and Santa was in the room with the huge wood-burning fireplace.

Mom greeted us and said that Santa had just arrived. Mom, Dad, Grandma, Samy, and I, walked toward "Santa's Room." It was just as majestic as the year before with its thirty-foot tree and fireplace. The smell of the wood burning and the evergreen tree said "Merry Christmas" to all who entered the room. Santa really did look like royalty seated on that enormous plush red velvet chair. Samy did not have to wait long to be granted his audience with Santa. He walked to the front of the red velvet rope and Santa turned and said "Merry Christmas, young man."

Samy was somewhat taken aback by Santa's immediate greeting however he calmly walked to Santa and said "Merry Christmas, Santa." They talked for a while and I photographed them from every possible angle.

Mom and Dad asked Samy what they talked about and it seemed like all Samy could say was "Santa is so nice. He asked me what I wanted for Christmas and I told him that we emailed him a list. Santa is so nice."

"Did you tell him some of the things that were on your list?" Mom asked.

"I think I told him everything!" Samy answered.

§

Grandma and Grandpa came over to where Samy and his parents were standing outside of Santa's Room. Grandma suggested that we go have some hot chocolate and that I would take some photographs near the main entrance. We took some photos and went outside to walk through the extravagantly decorated gardens. We did not expect that these fabulous gardens would put on the show that greeted us. Yes, it was snowing! Samy turned to everyone and said with the enthusiasm and excitement found only in a child at this special time of year, "Grandpa was right, it's snowing!"

"Can we go down the waterfalls and walk through the maze again, Mom?" Samy asked as he began catching snowflakes.

There are some times when saying "no" is not an option. This was one of those times. Samy led us down the steps that bordered the waterfall on his way to find the maze. The air remained quite crisp and the snow was adding to the magic of the evening.

Grandma and I persevered and were having as much fun watching Samy as he was touring the gardens. After an hour of watching their grandson and touring these magnificent gardens, Grandma and I told Samy and his parents we would meet them by the hot chocolate in the main building and headed back. We always knew why having children when you were young was a good idea, tonight just reaffirmed what we already knew. We watched the snow falling through the enormous windows and the reflection of the Christmas lights on the snow. The light snow enhanced the beauty of the evening and gave it that "crowning touch."

§

We were sitting in the main room when we detected Samy's unmistakable laughter coming through the dramatic rear doors of the building with his parents. Without wasting any time, he came over to us and said, "Grandpa let's go over by the train set and see if they added anything." I quickly agreed and we were off to the train room.

"Let's see if we can get some ideas for our layout," Samy said as we approached the train display. A model railroad club in the area constructed a display each year, which added to the charm of this already magnificent place. It featured a winter scene with an illuminated village, tunnels, and small-scale trains. Samy and I spent at least a half-hour looking at the trains. Our imaginations had never let us down and tonight was no different!

I was as enthusiastic as my grandson when it came to our latest adventure on what was proving to be a very interesting and worthwhile journey. While we were looking at the snow-covered mountain, I asked Samy, "What do you think of the mountain?"

"It looks good Grandpa but not as realistic or as tall as ours," Samy answered without the slightest bit of hesitation.

"Maybe we should share our mountain-building techniques with them, Samy" I replied.

"You mean our sculpture techniques, Grandpa," Samy said remembering how our mountain turned out to be more of a sculpture.

We walked over to Mom, Dad and Grandma who were sitting at a table and joined them for a delicious cup of hot chocolate. Was it possible that the snow made even the hot chocolate taste better? Samy and I agreed that tonight anything was possible!

"Will Santa will bring me everything on my list?" Samy said thoughtfully.

"Why do you ask?" His mother said genuinely interested in what prompted his question.

"I was thinking about all the boys and girls who really don't have much to play with and maybe they should get something for Christmas too." Samy stated with a concerned tone in his voice.

"It is your concern for these boys and girls that is precisely the reason Santa will make every effort to fill your list. You did a great job filling your shoebox and you even helped by giving some of the toys you don't play with anymore," Mom added.

§

We sat and marveled at how grand the gardens were and how happy we were that we had become aware of them. Samy's eyes were particularly wide tonight and when I looked at him, I wondered whether it was my perception that made his dimples so deep, his smile so charming, and his eyes so green. Some say that "you can never go back," and things will never be as good as we remember them. Our family had had "gone back" three times now and each visit was as memorable as the one before.

I desired only for Samy to go forward and grow, and he has in every way that matters. Samy and I were having a great time on our journey together. It has taken us back in time briefly to enjoy a simpler time in the past, but always to enhance the present and make the future just a little bit brighter! Tonight, as we left Santa and these spectacular gardens we did so without sadness but with happiness at having created another beautiful memory, and another "snapshot in time".

> *"Surely, two of the most satisfying experiences in life must be those of being a grandchild or a grandparent."*
>
> DONALD A. NORBERG

CHAPTER 26

The Latest Addition and "Expedition"

The Milwaukee diesel engine had been the focus of our attention the minute we saw it. Samy and I studied its history and marveled at how detailed it was. The Milwaukee had become the first engine to grace the tracks of the S&G Railroad and keep "Old Bob" company this past year. Last Christmas Santa left this beautifully detailed engine for Samy on Christmas morning. This Christmas Samy had asked for the Pennsylvania Berkshire Steam Engine. The Berkshire locomotive was a replica of one of the most powerful engines ever built. Highly detailed and all metal, this engine possessed museum quality details and features.

The Milwaukee diesel engine was on the top of Samy's Christmas list last year. The Berkshire steam engine was on the top of the list he had emailed Santa this year. Samy had done quite a bit of research before selecting this particular locomotive. We wanted to remain consistent and its authenticity and detail made it the perfect addition for our layout's time and geography.

It was Christmas Eve and as tradition dictated, we would be going to church and back to Samy's house for Christmas Eve Dinner. Samy's grandparents, aunts, uncles, and cousins would be there and he was looking forward to seeing them all. Samy was excited to see everyone, and play with his cousins. He enthusiastically helped a great deal when we played the "white elephant" present exchange. Samy possessed the ability to perform the mental equivalent of multi-tasking. During the white elephant game he whispered to me "Do you think Santa will leave the Berkshire steam engine?"

"You don't have long to wait, and I am as excited as you are to find out," I whispered back.

The evening passed by quickly and we soon found ourselves saying good-bye at the door. Samy gave us a huge hug, wished us a "Merry Christmas", and told us to call him in the morning.

"Call me in the morning and don't worry about waking me up," I said as I walked out the door.

"Oh I will Grandpa, I will," Samy answered with a tone in his voice that indicated I could definitely count on his call.

§

It had always been our custom to open presents on Christmas Day at Grandma and Grandpa's house, which was now less than a half mile away. Grandma and I considered this the best feature our subdivision had to offer. Location, location, location was replaced by Samy, location, Samy!

I awoke early Christmas morning and remembered getting up when I was Samy's age and racing to the Christmas tree to see what Santa had left for me. Had it really been that long since I was this enthusiastic about a Christmas present? The joy it would bring to my grandson surely had something to do with it. Something eerily familiar came over me when I thought about my grandson receiving a much-anticipated gift from Santa on Christmas morning.

The phone rang and I answered it on the first ring. Samy's voice was enthusiastically trying to articulate that Santa had indeed left the Pennsylvania Berkshire for him. My grandson is seldom at a loss for words and this morning was no different. Today there were just too many of them to get out all at once. The never-ending list of adjectives he was using to describe the present Santa had left for him was impressive to say the least.

"Grandpa, Santa brought me the Pennsylvania Berkshire with all of those features we saw. You won't believe how cool this engine is, it is so super-detailed and has more things like a whistle, headlight, two men inside, a bell, and..."

"That is tremendous Samy and I will be right over to see it," I said interrupting him.

I was genuinely interested in the train however judging from Samy's reaction it was more than the train that I wanted to see. I was at Samy's side examining the train within ten minutes. Samy was explaining all of the details to me. It was as if he had owned this scale model replica of the great Pennsylvania Berkshire engine for years. He was clearly ecstatic with his present from Santa and could not stop talking about all the features of this phenomenal new addition to our layout! He began his description of his new engine the moment I stepped into the house and how thrilled he was that Santa had left it for him.

"Are you sure you are happy with your choice of a steam engine?" I asked him.

"I'm more than happy, I'm super-happy, this is the coolest engine there is!" Samy immediately answered.

§

The next few days the Pennsylvania Berkshire thundered past the presents and decorations under Samy's Christmas tree. This powerful 2-8-4 locomotive would wait until the New Year before the mountain range and bridge of our layout tested its abilities. We fine-tuned our mountain pass to include a gradual grade through our mountain and a level run at the back of our upper level. We were certain that the features built in to this powerful locomotive would allow it to climb the upward grade of our mountain pass and negotiate the curve on to the Rockville Bridge.

Time passed by quickly and before we knew it, Samy and I were putting the Pennsylvania Berkshire engine and its cars on the track of their new home. Samy had expressed some concern about the new engine being able to climb the mountain pass we had designed because it was much heavier than the Milwaukee engine. We also had elevated our mountain slightly which made the section of track leading up to the mountain tunnel that much steeper.

"Here it goes, Grandpa," Samy said as he slowly raised the lever on the transformer. Immediately after Samy applied power to the track, we were listening to the "crew talk" coming from the engine and tender. Afterwards, we heard the "realistic" chuffing of the steam engine as the Berkshire picked up speed and easily climbed up to and through our mountain tunnel. "Wow, Grandpa, this engine climbs easily and when it reaches level track it runs so smooth," he said, clearly impressed with the performance of the S&G Railroad's most recent acquisition.

"You wouldn't think an engine that weighs as much as this one would be able to climb as easily as it does." Needless to say, I was very happy that everything had worked out so well and that Santa had come through for the S & G Railroad once again.

"The steam whistle, chuffing sounds, and the crew talk are really cool," Samy quickly added.

Two hours later, we had put the Pennsylvania Berkshire and all of its cars through our rigorous testing standards and it passed with "flying colors." It had now become worthy of joining the Milwaukee Diesel Engine and of course "Old Bob" on our layout! The almost four feet by four-foot addition to our layout gave us room for the rail yard to park any trains not in use. The switches we had installed also gave us the ability to cut power to the tracks in the rail yard while we ran trains on the main lines.

§

"Grandpa, I think it's time for another expedition for our rail yard." Samy said with a grin that indicated he was thinking about the next step we should take.

"What did you have in mind?" I said knowing that Samy was about to be forthcoming with a plan for what he was referring to as our next expedition.

"Do you remember when we went to the field near the woods where we found all those really cool rocks?"

"I sure do Samy, that was where we found that rock wall with the striated rock just the color we had in mind."

"We need some gravel for our train yard and I think I remember seeing some on the trail near the rock wall." The prospect of going on another "expedition" was exciting to both of us.

Samy did not have to wait long. I enjoyed our "expeditions" together as much as he did. They were always fun, educational, adventurous and sometimes mysterious. They were never boring. We always came back with stories to tell about our adventures that we were sure would amaze anyone who heard about them!

"Let's go now before it gets too late. We'll bring some small plastic bags with us in case we find some good gravel for the train yard." Samy quickly took some bags and we were on our way.

§

We walked toward the end of our subdivision and the hiking trails where our rock wall stood. It was a cool sunny day and Samy and I walked side by side talking about his soccer game, school, and of course the S & G Railroad. I could not help think how it does not get much better than this. Just being able to spend so much time with my grandson, who I loved very much, was truly a blessing and I thanked God every day for it.

We saw the rock wall about fifty yards in front of us and our pace quickened. We reached the wall and after carefully surveying the rocks surrounding it, we concluded that none was the type you would find in a railroad yard. Samy looked at me as if a light bulb went on and said, "Grandpa, I remember when we took that walk on the hiking trail near the stream there was a lot of small gravel and it's not too far."

"You lead the way, Samy and I will follow you." We walked another hundred yards or so and the hiking trail was in front of us, just as Samy remembered.

"Grandpa, look up ahead, I think I see the perfect gravel for our train yard," Samy said eagerly. I knew he could not wait to get there to complete our quest for the perfect gravel. I had walked this hiking trail many times before only today was quite different!

"This will look great Grandpa," Samy said as he sifted through the gravel carefully picking out only the small ones that would be suitable for our train yard.

"Samy, I think you found the perfect spot for gravel. This will look good, and it's tailor-made for us."

We put the carefully selected gravel in our bags and started home taking a few detours along the stream, searching for the many different treasures the woods and trails had to offer! At one point Samy spotted a particularly inviting spot on the stream that ran parallel to the trail we were on. Large flat rocks lined the base of the stream and it looked as though they may have fallen at one time down the steep grade on the other side. We could not resist exploring this part of the stream. The rocks acted like a bridge across the small rapids that hastened the flow of the stream. An hour had passed, and we were about to head home when we heard a "snap" as if someone on the far side of the stream had stepped on a branch. Sam looked up and said quizzically, "What was that, Grandpa?"

"I think there's a 'squatch' in these woods," I answered eerily.

"What is in these woods, Grandpa?" Samy said with a chuckle in his voice.

"Have you ever heard of 'Sasquatch'? Some people say it's a legend and others say they have seen these very tall creatures that resemble a bear but walk and look somewhat like a man."

"There is a show on the History Channel about these people who are looking for one. Do you think it's real, Grandpa?"

"There are a lot of people who do but I think there are many people who actually 'like' believing something exists for the fun and mystery that surrounds these stories. There was one guy who went through the trouble of renting a professional costume and running through the woods. He had someone video everything and the people who lived in this area were either afraid to go near the woods or went in to hunt for 'Bigfoot'. This lasted for a couple of years before the video was examined closely and declared a hoax. The man who staged everything finally admitted he did it just as a joke. This could have turned out badly and either he or someone else could have been shot. Since no one has caught one or even managed to catch one on a legitimate video, I find it very hard to believe they exist."

"That doesn't mean we can't tell Grandma that we saw one in the woods!"

Samy's characteristic sense of humor, which always seemed to put certain things in perspective, went into high gear. He began to laugh and could hardly finish his next sentence when I interrupted him.

"What are you thinking about that is so funny?" I loved it when Samy laughed and he repeated his question.

Samy regained his composure long enough to answer and said "I was thinking about Grandma when we tell her about Sasquatch."

"What about Grandma and Sasquatch?" I said trying to contain my laughter.

He was still laughing and said, "Grandma won't let us explore the woods or hiking trails anymore."

We headed home and found ourselves talking about all the humorous scenarios we could adapt to our "Bigfoot" stories, especially for Grandma. There was a bridge across the stream about halfway to our home and I pointed to it and said, "That tree would be a good place to put a sign that says 'Bigfoot Crossing'. What do you think, Samy?"

Samy laughed and said, "That would be a really cool idea, Grandpa!"

We arrived home with our rocks and gravel and Grandma reminded us that they we should thoroughly wash everything. She had told us once before and of course we found it quite humorous, when she said that animals might have gone to the bathroom on them. Grandma was right and we carefully scrubbed anything we put on our layout. That did not prevent us from teasing Grandma about the animals and our rocks. Today was different because we still had our "dangerous" Bigfoot stories to tell Grandma.

§

The day ended in much the same way all days I spend with Samy. He astonishes me with his intelligence, wit, personality, and sense of humor. His sense of wonder about the world around him allows his imagination to expand at every opportunity. Our time together is my most valued treasure! The "snapshots in time" we create are priceless and will remain in our hearts forever.

"Let every man be a master of his time."

WILLIAM SHAKESPEARE

CHAPTER 27

"𝕬 𝕷𝖎𝖋𝖊 𝖔𝖋 𝕴𝖙𝖘 𝕺𝖜𝖓"

Our journey together had spiraled into something neither of us had imagined. Every aspect of our layout presented us with challenges and opportunities we thoroughly enjoyed and our successes provided the motivation to progress even further. The research we completed served as a basis for much of what we have achieved. Our collective imagination provided the real substance for our achievement.

Several months ago we had ordered an assortment of miniature figures however when they arrived we found that even though they were the correct scale, they could not "stand" on their own. It was now time to bring our village area to life with the addition of our miniature people, our new trolley track, and our illuminated train/trolley station. Our first task was to create bases for our people. We glued them on to small squares of thin poster paper and painted the bases the same color as the surface they were standing on. Samy placed them carefully inside and outside of our buildings as well as on the train station.

"Grandpa, look at how real they look and they make everything come alive!" Samy said, genuinely impressed with the result obtained by the addition of the figures to our layout.

"Switch on the lights for the buildings and train station and they will look even more realistic."

Samy switched on the lights and we both stood back to admire our village and its people. Samy had meticulously placed the miniature people inside the stores, in front of the stores, about to cross the street, and on the train/trolley station as well.

§

In many ways, our town did have a life of its own and we knew it well. The research we had done told us when it was established and the effect the railroad had on its development. It was even more special because "we" had built it. Better still, we had modeled it after the town in which we live!

Our trolley was ready for the special ultra-thin black track we had purchased. The track blended with the street, ran in an oval pattern in front of our stores, and stretched from our town hall to our church. In the center was the illuminated platform where the towns-people waited for the trolley. Samy assembled the track from above and I wired the track to the transformer from below.

"This track looks so great, and the way it matches the street makes it look as authentic as the rest of our village," Samy said without taking a breath.

"I'm glad we thought ahead and gave the trolley its own power supply independent from the rest of the trains," I said as I crawled out from under the layout.

Samy agreed that the trolley should have a separate control, especially when it came to speed. The time had come to put out all the room lights, close all blinds and power on our switches that controlled our lighting.

"Here they go Grandpa," Samy said ceremonially as he flipped the switches and turned on our lighting. As he gradually gave the trolley power, its lights went on, and it cruised around the new track the same way it did at the turn-of-the-century!

"This is my favorite part when we finish doing some-thing and we stand back and just look at it," Samy said as we watched the trolley pass one building after another and go around the curve near the church."

"I couldn't agree with you more buddy, it gives you a real feeling of having accomplished something."

"Do you think we will ever be finished?" Samy said thoughtfully.

"I think the real question is do we want to be finished? We have done so much and had such a great time that I guess my answer would have to be no."

I had no doubt that Samy did not want our journey to end. There also was no doubt as to how long we wanted it to last! We were technically finished with all of the items on our original list and more, but somehow we always seem to think of more additions or improvements to our original plan.

"Let's do our pond, waterfall, and stream next, Grandpa."

"You forgot, they were marked as future development projects to be done at a later date..."

"Oh Grandpa... I think this is the 'later' date."

"Get over here you" I said as I chased Samy under the layout.

§

We ended up discussing how far we had come and as usual totally lost track of time. Samy again asked if we would ever be finished and I told him there was nothing I would rather be doing and that in some ways I hoped we would never be finished.

"I think I know what you mean Grandpa," Samy said thoughtfully.

There was no doubt in my mind that Samy did indeed know what I meant. Suddenly, we heard the sound of Mom and Dad's voices and it was clear they were looking for us. We adjourned our meeting and decided to show Mom and Dad what we had accomplished with our village. Samy's presentation describing to his mother and father all the miniature people, our new trolley track and illuminated train station was as good as a tour guide at the Smithsonian. He described each in detail pointing out that everything on our layout was authentic and period correct.

Mom and Dad were visibly impressed and when Samy finished his presentation, Mom said "Wow, this looks like a professional display!" Dad was equally impressed and said, "Everything you have done from the mountains, elevated track, bridge and now your village could be on the cover of a magazine!" Samy was beaming from ear to ear as he thanked his mom and dad. He continued to recall the memories we shared painting and grouting the buildings and how much fun the mountain was to build.

"We are going to build a waterfall on the mountain. The stream with two smaller falls will be right here." Samy went next to our mountain and pointed to the locations of the two smaller falls. He then pointed to the location where the large falls would come off the mountain at the end of the stream. "The waterfall will empty into a large pond below and we may even put a small rowboat with a family fishing, in the pond," Samy said with a great deal of enthusiasm.

"Now we are really impressed," his mother said reacting to Samy's overwhelming enthusiasm for what he was doing.

"Grandpa found this crystal clear caulk we are going to use for the stream and waterfalls and it really looks cool. It dries crystal clear and will look just like real water."

Mom and Dad's shared enthusiasm added to Samy's excitement and enhanced the experience. Samy was growing and learning more every day and his sense of wonder about the world around him, showed no signs of diminishing any time soon!

§

"Do you know what this reminds me of Samy?" Mom said.

"Do you mean building a waterfall, Mom?" Samy asked.

"Not a waterfall Samy, it was a two-story model house that Grandpa helped me build for a school project when I was about your age. It had windows in it, doors, and was even wired for small lights in each room."

"That sounds really cool mom, what was it for?" Samy asked.

"I'm not 100% sure what subject in school it was for but it was a project that was assigned to be done with a friend of mine. We decided to make it at my house and Grandpa offered to help us. We did the written report and your grandfather helped us with the actual building. Grandpa got so involved with the building that sometimes we had to tell him that we wanted to build."

"That was a really long time ago Mom, a really long time." Samy laughed and waited for a reaction from his mother, which he promptly received.

"You better watch it! You know it wasn't that long ago."

"It couldn't be ...you are only 28 now!" Samy replied diplomatically.

"By the time 'our' project was finished my friend and I had put dollhouse furniture we had in every room. Grandpa, on the other hand ended up putting working lights in each room, a doorbell, and many other things. I even think it had a chimney!"

"Sounds like Grandpa to me only now Grandpa lets me do everything!" Samy said proudly.

I admitted that I did remember the project and being carried away with the building of it!

§

Time passes quickly but some things never change. The excitement, involvement, and opportunities we are given last a lifetime. The more we are involved the more our desire to do more increases. It is true that "Nothing breeds success like success." It is also true that we do not succeed if we do not try. The more opportunities we are given the greater the likelihood we will indeed succeed.

I shared these sentiments and knew that the opportunities presented to Samy in the building of the S&G Railroad would benefit him by giving him these opportunities to succeed. I also hoped that the S&G Railroad would live on for generations. I was confident that Samy would someday pass on its history and the memories it created. Samy and I had created much more than a model railroad layout. Together we had created memories that would last forever and strengthen the bond between us. We learned much about the history of our town, country and the railroad. Perhaps most important of all, we learned much about our family and ourselves. The skills Samy used on our journey together would serve him well in the future. Perhaps someday, with his son or grandson, they will look back and create memories of their own.

Samy and I had become builders, historians, railroad experts, stoneworkers, bridge builders, archaeologists, explorers, sculptors, painters, geologists, mathematicians, and much more. We had visited local historical landmarks together and we knew our journey was just beginning! These were the "snapshots in time" that were most precious to both of us.

> "No pessimist ever discovered the secrets of the stars, or sailed to uncharted land, or opened a new doorway for the human spirit."
>
> HELEN KELLER

CHAPTER 28

"One For The Record Books"

Samy and I were in the backyard practicing with Samy's new golf clubs. I was attempting to give Samy some "pointers" on some of the fundamentals of the game such as the grip, stance, and swing. I knew from experience the frustration that this game very often presented, especially to those just starting out.

Samy listened as I showed him the proper grip and stance for each club. He was an extremely "quick study" and had no trouble remembering how to hold the club or where to stand when addressing the ball. Together we practiced all three fundamentals, hitting our whiffle golf balls from the front of the yard to the back. This was Samy's first time with the exception of miniature golf and his competitiveness helped him remain focused. We played in the yard for about two hours.

"Grandpa, we should go on another expedition," Samy said unexpectedly.

"Where exactly did you want to explore?" I said, caught somewhat by surprise.

"Do you remember the stream we followed past the tennis courts at the back of the hiking trail? I think we should follow that and see where the stream goes."

Samy and I remember being intrigued by the twists and turns the stream was making as it headed out of our subdivision. We also noticed the huge flat rocks that lined the stream were increasing in number as we hiked further. Samy had not forgotten and wanted to hike further downstream.

"I am ready if you are," knowing that there was no doubt that Samy would be.

§

"Expedition" had become synonymous with exploring places we had not been before. In the time it took to put away our golf clubs and collect the golf balls, Samy and I were on our next expedition. We chose the hiking trail that was closest, to the house to enter the woods on our way to an area beyond the tennis courts that we called "Flat Rock Point." It was here that we entered uncharted territory.

"Grandpa, look at the moss that is growing on the rocks in the riverbed. It's bright green and looks so healthy." Samy commented that they resembled the coral in his saltwater aquarium. I made a mental note to look up the type of moss we were seeing because Samy's observations about this moss were extremely accurate.

We had hiked this trail before however we had never gone this far. Everything on both sides of the stream was new to us and it appeared as if not too many people had been here before. The trail was far from "worn" and there were many times we had to climb over branches and trees that had fallen across it. My partner was not the least bit deterred by some of the obstacles we were encountering. As we progressed, the woods became denser and the trail began to disappear. We both observed the absence of any houses or man-made structures of any kind within sight. I gave some thought to turning back because the light filtering through the trees seemed to be fading. The last thing I wanted was for the two of us to get lost any more than we already were.

"Samy, do you want to call it quits for today?" I asked, realizing what a foolish question that was.

"Not yet Grandpa, come over here and look at the rocks in the stream! They look as if they change color when you look at them from a different angle and they are flat."

Sure enough, the rocks in the stream did appear to change color depending on how the light hit them. They were quite a bit larger than those we were accustomed to seeing on our expeditions through the woods. The woods themselves were quite a bit different than the wooded area closer to our home. Everything looked larger, denser and in some ways very intimidating.

"You are right about these rocks Samy, they are quite a bit different from the ones we usually see upstream. They are unique in the way they reflect light. We should name this part of the stream after you since you discovered the rocks."

"The stream looks like a big 'S' from here," Samy said as he was standing on one of the large flat rocks in the stream."

"That's it, Samy, the stream is shaped like the first letter of your name. I think it is only appropriate that we name this area 'Samy Bend'." We were now standing on the same huge flat rock together at the beginning of Samy Bend.

"Sounds good to me Grandpa," Samy said as he smiled at the idea of naming this part of our uncharted territory after him.

§

Further downstream, we saw a house in the distance that towered over us. Samy and I examined this house and saw that it stood on the precipice of what appeared to be a fifty foot cliff! The house resembled a castle. It was built entirely of stone and had a turret-like structure that curved upward the entire height of the right side of the house. The windows were recessed quite a bit and the third floor windows looked like small squares. There were no other houses or structures of any kind in any direction and we concluded that by its appearance this castle-like structure had been there a very long time. Samy reminded me of a book we had read together about castles in the Middle Ages and how some noblemen came to America at a time when it was no longer economically feasible to maintain their castles in Europe. They attempted to reproduce them here in America on a smaller scale. Could Samy be right? Was this one of those attempts?

"I don't think I would like to live there. It has no backyard and looks like it's going to fall off the cliff. I wonder if anyone lives there," Samy commented as he strained his neck upward.

"Maybe they built it that way for the same reason castles were built in the Middle Ages to keep out invaders." Samy laughed and we continued our journey downstream. We had left our subdivision far behind us and did not anticipate the surprise the stream was about to present us with. In the back of our minds was the ominous castle-like structure that we just passed. We agreed that we would do some research and perhaps contact the local historical society who may know of its existence or even the history of it.

One-hundred yards or so beyond the "cliff" the stream seemed to disappear. After hiking mostly uphill for quite a distance we discovered something that we were sure would make us turn back. Directly in front of us was a huge mountainous structure composed mostly of rock. It seemed to come out of the ground abruptly and was at least thirty feet tall. There were bushes, shrubs, and small trees growing between the dark-colored rocks that made this "mountain" seem threatening. Since it was so steep we immediately ruled out any climbing. Upon further investigation, we discovered that the stream we were following had split and virtually disappeared. This stream had been our guide and without it we would be lost...literally and figuratively! Was there a way around this monstrous landform we had encountered? Was the stream we were following on the other side? These were two great questions we wished we had the answers to.

I cautioned Samy to stay next to me as we went to investigate further. We discovered that the stream did split into two and went around both sides of what we were now calling "Monster Mountain". The woods and trees at the base of the mountain were so dense that it was impossible to see the streams until you were quite literally on top of them. The banks of the stream on the left were definitely too high to climb on the opposite side of the stream, so we walked up a "path" near the stream on our right. This path was steep compared to what we were used to, but compared to the mountain in front of us, it looked level! As we walked around our mountain we could see it was just as steep on the opposite side. In the distance we could see what appeared to be the beginning of a relatively new subdivision. We were definitely in uncharted territory, and we knew it.

"Are we lost yet Grandpa?" Samy asked with a grin on his face.

"What do you mean lost? I was a Boy Scout back in 1956 for at least a week!"

"Now I feel so much better," Samy said as he started to laugh.

"I thought you would. Now that you know my extensive wilderness training, you should feel much better." We both were laughing now as we continued to walk up the path on the right. We could now see the streams did become one again beyond the mountain.

The new subdivision was directly in front of us. All that separated us was a pond, the stream, and some very steep banks along the stream. As much as we wanted to we could not reach the banks of the pond. The ground was becoming softer the closer we got to the pond. We could tell that the swamp-like plants that were growing around the pond would prevent us from reaching it.

Perhaps on another day when we figured out exactly where we were we could approach this potential fishing hole from another direction. At the moment we had to deal with the large rocks that prevented us from climbing the banks of the stream. Although we had all of these intriguing and somewhat mysterious things in sight, we seemed to have hit a "dead end." The light was fading, the obstacles in our path were insurmountable and it looked like the only prudent course of action for us was to turn back.

It was only when we were about to turn back that Samy spotted something yellow through the trees. It was above us and at least 100 yards ahead. What could this be? We decided to forge ahead to get a closer look! Our decision proved to be a good one because after 25 yards we saw a large yellow bulldozer in the distance and what looked like a path or perhaps a future hiking trail under construction for this new subdivision. We still had to climb up the bank of the stream which became less steep as we reached our much welcomed construction vehicle. Samy and I followed the dirt path it had made and it led us to the beginning of a street that had been cleared for development. We walked down the "street" and based on my sense of direction only, I suspected our location, but there was certainly no way to be sure yet.

Together we walked over a bridge built over a stream that was at least five times as wide as the stream in our subdivision and was clearer and deeper than the one we had been following. This was something we had talked about many times, and wished we had in our subdivision. We wanted a pond or a stream capable of supporting fish so we could go fishing together.

§

"Grandpa, look over on the left there's a fish," Samy said excitedly. We paused for a moment next to the railings that lined the bridge to look down at the stream. Sure enough, there was a fish and another until we had counted a small school of about five fish!

I looked down the street and saw a pool and clubhouse that were still under construction. Certainly, there must be a sign that would help us determine exactly where we were. I walked over to a new sign and could hardly believe my eyes. The sign read "The Estates at Providence". I now knew for sure we were quite a distance from home!

"You are not going to believe where we are," I called to Samy who was still engrossed in the fish we had found. He was at my side in ten seconds and together we read the sign – twice! Samy was familiar with the location of this new subdivision because his father had done some work in the older section. The older section was almost two miles further from our present location and at least another mile to the main street the entrance was on.

"You told me a long time ago that if we traveled far enough in this direction we would end up here," Samy reminded me.

"You are right, but at the time I never thought we would hike this far through the woods," I answered still trying to process that it was over two years ago that I had told Samy that.

We started to walk up the newly-cleared street looking for the same path where we exited the woods. Lots were being cleared and utility lines buried for the new homes that would line this street in the not-to-distant future. The road turned to gravel bordered by forms for the new cement curbs that would soon be poured.

"The best way to get home is to go back the way we came. There's the bridge we came over when we came in," Samy said as he pointed to the street behind us.

"Have a look down this street, Samy." He walked over to where I was standing and sure enough, there was an identical parallel street and bridge.

"Which way do we go now Grandpa?" Samy said somewhat concerned.

"You look worried, Samy," I said.

"I have soccer practice today at seven and Daddy likes to get there at six-thirty."

"I'm sure we will be back with time to spare," I assured him.

§

We now had to make a choice between two identical bridges with the same black iron railings in an area we knew nothing about. This was as far as we had ever hiked together and Samy and I hoped our choice would lead us back to the trail we had taken.

"Do you remember how high the first street was? It was on the edge of the subdivision and I am pretty sure we turned left at the first street," I said as I looked down both streets.

"You're right Grandpa, I remember the street sign we were trying to read from far away!" Samy's somewhat concerned look now turned to excitement.

"It seems like we now have a plan and a way to retrace our steps."

"We sure do Grandpa, we sure do" Samy answered looking very relieved.

We reentered the woods at the same place we had exited them and began to remember certain "landmarks" such as fallen trees, Monster Mountain, Samy Bend, the castle built on the cliff, and the shape of certain rocks we had seen. When we approached our castle-like house made entirely from stone we paused for a moment to take a closer look. The "castle" appeared to be quite old and was in a very remote area. There were no signs that anyone was living there but there was no way to be sure. We agreed that our focus should be on getting home. The "castle" would have to wait for another day.

"Grandpa this is our longest hike ever. This one was longer than the one we took with Mom and Dad in the mountains," Samy exclaimed as he hopped over a large bump in the trail.

"The biggest difference between that one and this one is the Mountain hike had a clearly marked trail with signs telling you where to go, Samy."

"We could use a few signs on this hike Grandpa," Samy said after pausing for a moment.

"Our signs are our landmarks that we remember, so keep looking for anything familiar you might recognize."

Samy and I were moving quickly through the woods that day and now that we recognized a few landmarks, we were confident we were heading in the right direction. Our pace began to quicken and Samy navigated the turns in the trail like an experienced hiker and showed no signs of tiring.

"Samy, look ahead and you will be able to see the top of the tennis court fence."

"Grandpa, I can see it now!" Samy was high enough on the trail to see this very important landmark. Our pace quickened and we sailed over the moss-covered "steps" we had discovered that were formed by tree roots.

§

The tennis court fence was a particularly significant landmark because it was located at the very back of the subdivision we lived in. On any given day a hike to the tennis courts on the hiking trails from our home was substantial. Today, it meant we were home. We were now standing behind the tennis courts at the very back of our subdivision.

"Any other day a hike to where we are now would be pretty far, and we are not going to forget this one for a long time!"

"This really was one for the record books, Grandpa."

Samy and I were no longer concerned about the time. We walked the rest of the way home talking about how completely "blown away" we were when the stream made an "S" and disappeared, the "castle" on that super-high cliff, Monster Mountain, the pond, and how we felt when we read that sign revealing our location. We had finally discovered that there were fish where the stream widened and wished for a pond close by so we could go fishing. Perhaps on another expedition we would find one!

In the course of our conversation, there were a few things we both agreed upon. The first was the castle and how we would have liked to get closer to investigate this ominous structure. The second was the pond and last but not least was what we referred to as Monster Mountain! Perhaps sometime in the future we would go on another "expedition" and unlock some of the mysteries they held. We were content with our memories of this expedition and looking forward to unlocking these mysteries was an adventure unto itself!

We reached the end of the hiking trail and could see our final destination. Mom and Dad were just arriving to pick up Samy. They spotted us at the entrance to the hiking trail and pulled the car up to where we were standing. Samy opened the back door and hopped into the car. We wanted to share our experience immediately with Mom and Dad however, we had so much to tell about our adventure that we simply did not know where to begin. Our timing could not have been better. Samy was happy he would not be late for practice and we had taken a hike that was surely, as Samy put it, "one for the record books."

§

Our latest "expedition" was one we did not plan but one we definitely will not forget! Our record-breaking hike that day took its rightful place among the many "snapshots in time" we will remember always.

"Adopt the pace of nature: her secret is patience."

RALPH WALDO EMERSON

CHAPTER 29

Patience and Imagination

ew things in this world capture the fascination of people more than a waterfall. If you ask someone, why he or she loves waterfalls so much, most will pause before they answer. The fact is waterfalls have a mesmerizing effect on all of us. They stimulate all of our senses and increase our appreciation of nature in its purest form. There are tens of thousands of waterfalls scattered throughout the world and each is unique in its own special way.

Samy and I were fortunate to have seen some of these while visiting the western part of North Carolina. We have discovered some small waterfalls on our recent expeditions through the woods near our home. It seemed logical that we include waterfalls on our train layout. When we built our mountain range we made sure, we had a mountain stream that would include two small water-falls and a large waterfall that would empty into the large pond or lake we planned to have.

"Grandpa, are we ever going to build the waterfall?" Samy asked impatiently.

"There were several ways we could build a waterfall," I reminded Samy.

"We could buy that kit Mom saw in the hobby store," Samy suggested.

"If we purchase the kit from the hobby store Samy, it would be faster but not go as far. In other words we would probably end up with less than half the amount of water than we planned and not be as realistic."

"How do we do it if we don't use the waterfall kit?" Samy said looking somewhat confused.

"The same way we built the mountain, tunnels, elevated track, our bridge, and the rock walls ... we use our creativity and imagination."

"I think I know what you mean but the waterfall is different," Samy responded with a very quizzical look on his face.

I was standing next to the mountain counting the places that were suitable for building waterfalls. Somewhere between one and nine I realized that the problem Samy was having with the waterfall had nothing to do with the placement of them but with the material used to simulate water.

"Have you ever heard of 'brainstorming'?" I said as I turned toward Samy.

"We did that even before we stared our layout, didn't we Grandpa?"

"We sure did Samy," I said proudly and very happy that my grandson had remembered.

Brainstorming could mean many things however, on this day Samy remembered that it was a way of coming up with ideas on how to do something. In this case, it was how to make something. I suspected that Samy had been thinking of a material to use for quite some time. I suggested that we each make a list of materials that looked like water or better still just name a few.

Just as we were about to begin, Samy's characteristic smile and enthusiasm returned and he said, "Grandpa, we can't use real water or anything that stays wet, so we have to use something that will dry and still look wet."

"How about that hair gel your mom puts on your hair?" I said.

"O h Grandpa, I really don't think so!" Samy said without any hesitation whatsoever.

"O.K. then how about glue that dries clear," knowing that Samy would reject this idea because it was far from three dimensional.

"It has to look like real water and we have to be able to almost see through it just like water. Not only does it have to look like water but we should be able to make it white like rushing water."

"Are you picturing it in your mind or are you trying to remember something you saw somewhere?" I asked Samy this as I observed him trying very hard to come up with a solution.

"Both" Samy answered, only this time there was a sparkle in his eyes that bordered on amusement. "I can't believe I did not think of this before...this will look so great!"

I had seen this light bulb come on before and experience had taught me to let Samy share what he had come up with as a solution to our waterfall problem.

"Do you want to share what you thought of with me?"

The fact that Samy was smiling and somewhat proud of himself for thinking of a solution was obvious and he repeated, "I really can't believe I didn't think of this before...we should use caulk, you know the clear kind!"

"That is a great idea, Samy...No it's better than great - it's fantabulous!"

"Thanks Grandpa, I can't think of anything that would work better." The look on his face now was almost one of relief. The same look you might see after solving a difficult math problem.

§

"I really don't think there is a better material to use so your idea is awesome!" I congratulated Samy again for coming up with a solution to our waterfall problem. The solution to the "water problem" was suddenly very clear. What we needed was caulk that was "crystal clear."

I was extremely proud that Samy had used his imagination the way he did. Samy had visualized the water, asked questions, and was able to see the possibilities his creative problem-solving skills provided him. The time had come to see if our waterfall caulk was available at any of the local stores. Checking online had become a reflex action and Samy headed for the computer.

"What would we do without the computer?" I considered the question exceptional as most children Samy's age simply took it for granted, the same way I thought about television when I was growing up.

"We would have spent more time at the library and in this case we would have to call or go to the store more often."

Samy paused for a moment, and said, "I know you didn't have computers when you were my age, so how would you look something up the way we have been doing on the computer?"

"When you wanted to know the meaning of a word you would look in a dictionary. If you were researching a particular topic or event many people had encyclopedias which came in sets from A-Z. Not everyone had these because a good set was expensive," I added.

"So if you didn't have a set of encyclopedias you went to the library."

I knew that Samy liked to go to the library and he did not consider this alternative such a bad one. In fact, he would probably consider a trip to the library to do research on our trains an "expedition!"

"I am sure of one thing Samy, the computer can be a very convenient and valuable resource if it's used the way we are using it. It can also be a great way for me to brag about my grandson by sending photographs of your soccer games."

§

We had a few thousand results for our search for clear caulk on the screen. To limit the number of results we went to "HomeLowes" site. As we scrolled through the pages of clear caulk, we found one that said "crystal clear" in the description. We had found the only caulk that would dry so you could see through it like a pane of glass.

"It looks like we are ready to go and I will pick up a few tubes tomorrow to have on hand. This way we will have it ready when we start the falls. The idea to use caulk was a good one and now that we located "crystal clear" caulk it is even better."

"Grandpa, I really never thought our layout was going to be so big and have so many things on it," Samy said thoughtfully.

"I never did either, Samy. We have come a long way and remember we did build it all!"

I looked toward Samy and thought about how fortunate I was. Samy actually enjoyed spending time with me and the feeling was mutual. We had come a long way and shared many adventures together and my instincts told me there were many more to come. Although the immediate task was to complete the waterfall, I had learned that some of the best "snapshots in time" I shared with Samy were those that were spontaneous and had nothing to do with what we were doing at that specific moment.

§

Samy was examining the largest site of our three waterfalls when he looked awayfrom the computer. He had come to a conclusion based on his research that "Waterfalls like ours don't really slide down the mountain. Most of them fall away from the mountain."

Samy was of course referring to the force of the water that made the waterfall put some distance between the water and the cliff over which it was cascading.

"That is a good observation Samy. We have to come up with a solution to hold the caulk away from the mountain in order for it to look realistic. Do you have any ideas on how we could accomplish this?"

"We could bend a piece of thin cardboard and put the caulk on that but you wouldn't be able to see through it."

"You are on the right track Samy. We need a material that would replace your cardboard idea and still allow us to see through it." At that precise moment, I felt I knew not only what Samy was thinking but also how he would inevitably arrive at a solution. Yes, I had that much confidence in his creative ability.

"I'll be right back," Samy said as he crawled under the layout to look through a box of miscellaneous supplies we kept for future use. He came back out with a grin from ear to ear and a treasure trove of supplies. These included the clear plastic "blister packages" from some of the items we had purchased. Holding what he considered the solution to our immediate problem in his hand he said proudly, "These should work Grandpa."

"Why do you think these will work?" I said as I looked at the material he had brought out from our supply box.

"The pieces of plastic are different from the cardboard because you can see through them and they are thinner," Samy said enthusiastically and with a great deal of confidence that this material would work.

Samy impressed me not only by what he had found, but with the confidence he exhibited when he described why they would work. I had seen this often in my grandson when the proverbial light bulb went on.

"This looks like the solution to our problem. Great job, Samy, we should cut it to size, make a bend at the top to hold it away from the mountain, and we should have a very realistic waterfall. How did you remember the plastic was there?"

"At first I didn't remember the plastic was there but I was picturing the caulk on the cardboard and how you couldn't see through it. When I saw the plastic pieces in the box and I was sure we could use them instead."

"So you did what we have talked about. You pictured the falls in your mind, thought of alternatives, and used your imagination to come up with a solution," I said knowing that Samy was growing in every way. Samy was extremely pleased with his solution and I knew this was a small step in a much bigger picture.

"The only thing we have to do now is make a small curve at the top of each of the backings for our waterfalls."

"How are we going to make a bend in the top of the plastic?" Samy asked.

"Since you have been so creative when it comes to solving our problems I thought I would leave that to you. I will however give you a few hints and you tell me if you think they will work," I added as I saw that Samy was taking this as a challenge much like the expeditions we had taken.

"O.K. Grandpa how do we bend the plastic without breaking it?" Samy asked.

"Today so much is made out of plastic and there are so many shapes and sizes. One of the ways they do this is the same method we used to make our rocks, only they use plastic."

"Just like our rock molds only instead of plaster they use plastic. How do they do that since our plaster was a liquid?"

"Think about it for a minute. If we want something to conform to the shape of our mold, than whatever that material is....

Samy responded excitedly, "It has to be a liquid."

"Do you remember by any chance what I told you about the glue we used on the buildings and how they worked?"

"The glue melted the plastic parts and that's it Grandpa, we have to melt it!" Samy answered without any hesitation.

"Excellent, Samy but with these plastic sheets it won't be as hard as you might think. They are very thin and the heat from a hair dryer should do the trick."

We measured the respective heights of our waterfalls and cut the height and width, adding two inches on the height to allow for our bend. After gluing them in place, we used our crystal clear caulk on sheets of wax paper for easy removal, to make our waterfalls. We gave the caulk the appropriate artistic touches with white paint to simulate the foaming effect of rushing water. Where the water entered the lake below, large ripples dominated the bottom at the point of contact, and gradually smaller ones as you moved away from the falls. We even used very thin pieces of cotton to simulate the mist at the bottom of our larger falls. The reveal would have to wait until the next day to allow everything to harden and dry properly.

§

When we returned that next day, we were not quite ready for the outstanding results we found. The caulk had dried crystal clear, the ripples looked great, and the mist looked just like the real thing. Overall, our waterfalls looked extremely authentic. As tradition dictated, we stepped back and admired our work.

"We have really outdone ourselves this time!"

This was one of the rare occasions Samy appeared speechless. Samy shook his head, and said "Grandpa, this was really worth waiting for."

These "snapshots in time" are priceless on so many levels. They create memories that will remain in our hearts and minds forever. We had completed all of the projects we had planned but we were sure we were not yet at the end our journey together.

"Twenty years from now you will be more disappointed by the things that you didn't do than by the ones you did do. So throw off the bowlines, sail away from the safe harbor, and catch the trade winds in your sails. Explore. Dream. Discover."

MARK TWAIN

CHAPTER 30

Memories and "The Big Reveal"

When I awoke the next day, I went to my office to check email and straighten up my desk. Waiting for my computer to wake up as well was not among my favorite things. I took the time to walk down the upstairs hallway and look at the "work of art" my grandson and I had created together. Memories of that first day when we went into the old master bedroom closet to set up our clubhouse flooded my mind. I never thought that day, over two years ago, would have led to where we were now.

We had created a beautiful layout together and more importantly, memories I was sure would last forever. Our "journey" together thus far, was filled with so much more than setting up a train layout.

Samy had suggested that after we straightened up, cleaned the tracks, and made sure everything was in perfect working order we should have a "reveal" for all to see. His wide-eyed enthusiasm had been the driving force behind our accomplishments, and today was no different. The knowledge that our journey would never end, combined with our creativity made what we had accomplished very rewarding.

§

"Are you ready for the big reveal?" I said as Samy walked through the door. The word reveal had finality to it that neither of us wanted to hear, but we assured each other that this was certainly not the end of our journey.

"More than ready, Grandpa, I think we should start by cleaning the tracks." Samy approached our plan with his usual enthusiasm that was contagious to those around him. Today was the day we were both waiting for. We would have the opportunity to highlight the results of our efforts. It was a significant landmark in our journey together.

§

Samy and I took all of the trains off the layout and lined them up neatly against the wall for cleaning. This included "Old Bob" and the original cars that came with the set, back in 1950. We had not decided where yet, but we had decided to give "Old Bob" a place of honor.

Using the track cleaning solution, we started to clean the significant amount of track our layout now possessed. Samy's thoroughness had always impressed me and today was no different. He did not miss a millimeter of track and constantly checked the cloth he was using for signs of residue that came off the track, turning the cloth frequently. He made sure the track that was enclosed by our tunnels was not neglected as well. Samy was cleaning the track next to our mountain when he looked at me and asked "Do you remember when we were building our mountain?"

"Of course, that was one of our 'crowning' achievements."

The mountain we created remained very special to both of us. The reason Samy gave was that we literally created it out of nothing but scraps of lumber, screening, and plaster. It seemed like only yesterday that we were wrapping the screening around the skeleton of the mountain and forming the ridges and streams. I remember how Samy had taken over the plastering and displayed considerable creative ability.

Samy was behind the village cleaning the upper section of track thoroughly.

"Grandpa, the way the track passes by the back doors of our village is just the way it should be. A train could unload supplies to any of them just the way they do now." He stopped for a moment to position a small truck near the back garage door of one of the buildings.

"I am going to go under the layout to check the wiring and make sure everything is secure. The last thing we want is for one of our connections to be loose during our reveal."

"Make sure you don't tape our 'cornerstone'," Samy said as I crawled under the layout. He could not possibly know how important those words written over two years ago were to me...or could he? The words written with black magic marker read "Samy and Grandpa 2010". Had two years really passed so quickly? In any event, it was important to me that Samy had remembered.

"Don't worry our 'cornerstone' will be here so you can show your grandson."

§

Two hours later, we were finished cleaning the track and all of the trains. "Old Bob" merited special attention and was oiled and greased as well as cleaned. We applied a special cleaner and polish to the other engines and rail cars. The layout looked tremendous and we thought it was better than any we had come across in our research.

"Do you know what I liked the best about doing this? The expeditions we took were so much fun and they helped us a lot," Samy said. I hoped, he would look back on these expeditions and perhaps take his son or grandson on expeditions of their own. Only then would Samy really understand how important they were to me. Samy recalled almost every detail of our successes and failures with stunning accuracy.

"I absolutely loved the expeditions we took. You are right they did help us. They gave us a lot of ideas and opportunities to use our imagination. The one thing that I liked best was spending time with you." I could not have been more serious and planned to take a lot more of what Samy and I referred to as "expeditions".

"We are getting closer," Samy said as he painstakingly positioned the miniature people in just the right positions near the stores.

"Close to what?" I asked.

"To the grand opening of the S&G Railroad," Samy replied as he positioned a figure on the steps of the Post Office. He smiled and placed another figure near the door to the restaurant and methodically worked his way up the main street of our village. The train station that was in the center of our village square was next on Samy's list. He positioned the miniature people on the platform meticulously as if they were waiting for the train or trolley. Samy was right the people did bring our village to life. They also brought the memories of every minute we spent researching our trains, village, people, and the period they lived in to life.

"You are doing an extremely good job with everything! The layout looks like a professional display and you should be as proud of yourself as I am of you." There was no exaggeration everything did look that good!

"Thanks, Grandpa, the layout really looks cool but I think we have two add a third level and a taller mountain on the opposite side of the table."

"That's all? How about putting an addition on the house approximately 20 feet wide and 25 feet long with twenty foot ceilings to allow us to fly remote control airplanes to an airport on our layout?"

Samy and I both laughed. When we looked at the clock, we could not believe we had been working for over four hours. It was getting dark and we had not positioned the vintage cars or street lamps we had.

"Time always seems to go fast when we work on the trains or go on expeditions," Samy commented. Samy's observation about time passing quickly was an understatement. More often than not, we found ourselves running out of time because we had the uncanny habit of trying to do more than we planned.

Going off on a tangent, often seemed the only logical thing to do.

§

"You do know what they say about time passing quickly? It is said that time goes fast when you are having fun!" We learned early in our journey together that learning was having fun. Building our mountains, tunnels, and scenery was not work but enjoyable. Our research was not boring but stimulating!

"Grandpa, I think that everything we did was fun. The painting of the building trim took us a long time but now when I look at them, I'm glad we did it." Samy held his right wrist with his left hand as if to support it. "Just remembering how slow and careful we had to be gives my wrist an ache," Samy said remembering that day painting the trim on the Victorian buildings we had assembled. Samy evidently remembered how torturously slow the painting was.

Samy chuckled to himself as he was re-positioning one of the people on the platform and I asked him if he was thinking about something funny.

"When I was fixing the lady waiting for the trolley I thought about Grandma when we got back from one of our expeditions." Just hearing my grandson say "expeditions" made me smile.

"And...," I said waiting for Samy to share.

"It was the time when we were talking about 'Bigfoot' or 'Sasquatch' and when we got home we found Grandma waiting on the front porch. She was worried about us. We told her we thought we saw 'Bigfoot' in the woods and..." He began to laugh so hard that it was difficult not to laugh with him. Of course telling dangerous "Bigfoot" stories to Grandma was something particularly hysterical to both of us!

§

We shared many stories about building our layout together. Our journey was based on recreating a simpler time in America during the building of the railroads. We found ourselves traveling back in time to the turn of the century, the 1950s and into the future.

We have had the "time of our lives" and do not intend to stop now. Samy and I agreed, that our journey together thus far, has been an educational and enjoyable experience we will never forget. Our imaginations made a time machine unnecessary and rendered the "flux capacitor" useless. Our commitment to our goals kept us on a steady course and helped us navigate through difficult times. We are by no means at the end of our journey together!

§

We have created many very special memories. These "snapshots in time" will remain in our hearts forever. Samy and I will always remember that it is truly "the journey, not the destination that is important!"

"To laugh often and much; to win the respect of intelligent people and the affection of children...to leave the world a better place...to know even one life has breathed easier because you have lived. This is to have succeeded."

RALPH WALDO EMERSON

§

Conclusion

his was just the beginning of an extremely powerful journey that we both hope will never end. It will extend infinitely beyond the boundaries of this and the books that follow. Our journey has taken us to places we previously never imagined and we have accomplished things we never thought were possible. It is our sincere hope that our incredible journey will inspire you to create one of your own.

Our children and grandchildren deserve nothing but your best. The schools cannot possibly hope to provide the time, love, patience, skill and understanding a parent or grandparent is able to. Your life experiences and unique position in the life of a child qualifies you to supplement the traditional classroom experience in ways every teacher only dreams they could. You are the most valuable member of a team whose sole purpose is to provide opportunities to enhance the mental, physical, and spiritual growth for the most important people in our lives. The next generation awaits your inspirational, valuable guidance and support.

It is incumbent upon all of us to make a difference in our children's lives. In a broader sense, the future of our entire world depends on us doing so. Our children face an extremely complex world with many negative influences in it. There is no greater cause we can champion, and no more noble effort we can dedicate ourselves to, than preparing our children for the challenges that lie ahead.

"Each generation goes further than the generation preceding it because it stands on the shoulders of that generation. You will have opportunities beyond anything we've ever known."

RONALD REAGAN

Who among us would not agree that our first priority should be our children and grandchildren? Look into a child's eyes, and you will see hope for the future. Share an experience or create a memory with them, and your confidence in their potential deepens. Their values and strength of character are a direct reflection of the immediate world that surrounds them every day. There is perhaps no loftier goal than making sure that the teachings and influences on our children provide them with every opportunity they deserve to grow and develop into productive members of society that will make this world a better place for each of them and for all of us.

Never doubt, not even for a millisecond, that you can make a difference. You can and you will! Your influence goes far beyond what the traditional learning environment can provide. Your time is the most valuable gift you can give. We all know time passes much too quickly and none of us has heard of anyone regretting "They should have spent more time at the office."

What is certain is that the positive influence we have on our children now will make the time you spend with them an enjoyable, educational, and productive experience. As parents, grandparents, and other caring adults, we know there are no guarantees when it comes to the human experience. If this is so, then it is even more imperative that we do as much as we can to help our children grow and develop.

The encouragement of a "can do" attitude for every young person is essential if they are to become successful pursuing their dreams. The very idea that some people are destined for greatness or are born to succeed is based on myth not fact. The failures we experience in life are only temporary setbacks on the road to achieving our dreams. Many people have given up because they did not know how close to achieving their goal they were. Instill that in your children and you will be halfway to achieving your goal of giving the children in your life an advantage they cannot buy or learn anywhere!

§

We encourage you to visit us at: sgintime.com for updates and photos about the creation of The S & G Railroad. We welcome your feedback and perhaps sharing your experiences with us as well! Our journey continues............!

About The Author

obert Michaels was a teacher in the New Jersey public school system for over thirty years. Throughout his award-winning career, he had always maintained that students learn best when they become involved. Two United States Presidents, three New Jersey Governors, local parent-teacher organizations, and various local and state officials recognized the programs and activities he created.

Mr. Michaels originally created an energy conservation project for alternative energy sources, and his seventh and eighth graders went on to compete against high schools and colleges in their state and won! Governors Brendan Byrne and Tom Kean recognized them for their excellence.

Secretary of State General Colin Powell cited Mr. Michaels as a tremendous example of how "Volunteerism in America" can make a difference. This project was born out of a need for more technology in the classroom. Collaborating with such companies as Lucent Technologies (AT&T), and many others in the private sector, he and his students turned an empty storage room into a computer stock room. One class – One teacher did make a difference!

Mr. Michaels was born and raised in New Jersey and currently lives with his wife in North Carolina. He has two adult daughters and one grandson who also live in North Carolina. Although he has never lost his love for teaching, he has now turned the focus of his considerable talent to writing. His "Snapshots in Time" series is one all parents, grandchildren, and grandparents will identify with and enjoy!

§

sgintime.com

Made in the USA
Lexington, KY
30 November 2013